THE
TWELFTH
OF
AUGUST

THE TWELFTH OF AUGUST

The Story of Buford Pusser

By W. R. MORRIS

AURORA PUBLISHERS, INC.
NASHVILLE/LONDON

"On the twelfth day of August, they shot Buford and his wife,

On the twelfth day of August, darlin' Pauline lost her life."

This book is dedicated to
Carolyn, my wife;
and
Angel Lea, Crystal Dawn and
Montica Renea

Acknowledgments

Most of the material in this book is the result of interviews with the persons directly concerned; the rest is either from personal observation or from official records.

The names of almost everyone who provided me with information are mentioned within the book, and for this reason, I will not identify them here.

However, there are certain persons whose contributions to my work are special: Mrs. Estelle Morris, my mother, whose help during the writing of the book was invaluable; also, J. D. Swartz, Mr. and Mrs. Ed Weaver and Justine; Charlie B. Smith, and Don C. Horton.

WRM

CONTENTS

Introduction

Buford Pusser is hardly believable, even as a legend.

At the age of thirty-two, he has been shot eight times, stabbed seven, rammed with a car, has watched his wife die in an ambush slaying, wrestled a bear, survived a grinding car crash and killed two persons.

The six-foot-six, two-hundred and fifty-pound McNairy County, Tennessee, sheriff has become a living monument to justice—casting across the state one of the tallest shadows in the history of law enforcement.

Sheriff Pusser's fame spread beyond McNairy County on August 12, 1967, when his blonde wife, Pauline, was killed in a hail of bullets which also critically wounded him.

His narrow escapes from death have inspired three ballads and the writing of reams of newspaper and magazine articles, and have made his life movie and television material.

Bing Crosby Productions have announced plans for a movie on the sheriff's life, and the American Broadcasting Company is considering a TV series.

In 1969, Tennessee Jaycees named Buford Pusser one of the state's "Outstanding Young Men" for his relentless pursuit of law and order.

W. R. Morris, author (left) with Buford Pusser.

Legends feed and grow on violence and sudden death. Both have shrouded the life of Buford Pusser.

When he first pinned on the sheriff's badge, a mile-long strip of cheap dives, gambling joints, and houses of prostitution, peopled by bootleggers and cutthroats, straddled the state line between McNairy County, Tennessee, and Alcorn County, Mississippi.

Murders were committed regularly on the strip, which was a stopping-off point for hoodlums hiding from the law. Tourists constantly complained of being robbed, and weighted bodies were often found in the nearby Tennessee River.

Activities on the line began slowing down in 1964 when Buford Pusser became sheriff of McNairy County. He launched a cleanup campaign which eventually rid the area of the gangsterlike element which had flourished there.

The state-line war left its battle marks on the young sheriff, however, and today, his wire-mesh jaw, the gift of plastic surgeons, barely moves when he speaks. A long purple scar runs across his face, and he has undergone six facial operations since the morning of August 12, 1967.

He dresses neatly—in tailored suits, white shirts, colorful ties, and well-shined shoes. Under his coat, on an alligator belt, he wears a holstered .357-caliber magnum pistol, part of his daily dress.

I have known Buford Pusser for more than three years. I have ridden with him on the back roads of McNairy County while he checked beer joints and dance halls. I have relaxed with him in his modest Adamsville home and occasionally I have enjoyed an evening of entertainment with him in a Memphis night club.

I have studied the man and have seen both the good and the bad. Without question, Buford Pusser is genuine—a rare commodity among men.

W. R. MORRIS

CHAPTER I

"Not Again!"

McNairy County Sheriff Buford Pusser rubbed his eyes until they hurt, then wrapped his fingers tightly around the steering wheel of his Ford XL, as the red needle on the dashboard quivered near the hundred-mile-per hour mark. He glanced at the clock on the dash—2:30 A.M.—. "Two more miles and I'm home," he said outloud. It was Saturday, and he had been awake for thirty hours; Saturday night was always hard, keeping the night spots under control, watching the drunks on the highway, patrolling all of the lonely corners of the county. There'd probably be a knifing, he thought, and his mind caught the flash of a blade and a young man doubling over in pain. It was an image he saw again and again, but now he pushed it out of his mind, trying to keep the souped-up Ford on the road. He wanted to be home, but most of all, he wanted to sleep.

The big car rocked slightly as it sped through the

darkness, clinging to the white line in the center of the road. Pusser brought a hand up to the top of his head and smoothed back his light brown hair, cut close to the scalp. He felt his eyelids droop and jerked his head savagely, locking his eyes on the highway. Then he let them wander briefly—to the thickly wooded slopes softly illuminated by the moon along the road that linked Selmer to Adamsville. He heard a hound, the howl distinct in the crisp October air. The sessions in circuit court had been unusually long that day and then there had been the patrolling and now the fatigue. If he could just sleep for a second.

Suddenly, but easily, the car nosed off the shoulder of the road, and the right front fender struck an embankment. The car shot high in the air and flipped over. As it crashed on its top, burrowing deeply into the mud left by rain the previous evening, the sound of twisting metal and breaking glass shattered the predawn silence.

Pusser was trapped inside the car. Pain shot through his left cheek where blood flowed from a deep gash and spilled over his face. He reached for the pain and felt his left eyeball hanging loose. Blood was coming fast. He found a pressure point, pressed hard and held back the flow.

He tried unsuccessfully to open the car door. There was the smell of gasoline dripping steadily from the car tank and meaningless sounds from the police radio. The aerial had snapped, cutting off contact with the dispatcher's office. With his free hand, he felt his face to see how much of it was still there. It was a face that plastic surgeons had spent months rebuilding; now the wire-mesh jaw sagged loosely away from it.

Almost an hour had passed when Pusser heard the sound of an approaching car. He waited, unable to raise his voice, but praying that the car would stop. Then there was the sudden screech of brakes. Apparently, the bright headlights had outlined the scattered debris on the highway. Then, out of the night, a young voice screamed;

"Oh, my God! It's Buford Pusser. Not again!"

The license plate—SHERIFF-50—had told the boy what he feared even before he saw Pusser trapped in the twisted wreckage of the car. For a fleeting second, he thought McNairy County's sheriff was dead. But then a whisper-soft voice in a Southern drawl said, "Would you please put out your cigarette? Gas is leaking everywhere." The same voice quickly and calmly asked the boy to drive to Adamsville, notify the police, and have a wrecker sent. The teen-ager scrambled quickly up the bank and in a moment, Buford heard the car leaving.

He was alone again. Would the boy panic? he wondered. There was nothing to do but wait.

After what seemed like an eternity, he heard an ambulance coming. For a fleeting moment, in his mind the far-away whine of the siren became the same sad cry he had heard another day. The unhappy memory of that day now came flooding back, and he felt again the emptiness he had known when he realized that his wife was dead, that the bootleggers, gamblers, whores and cutthroats he had long battled had murdered her and left him, sprawled over the steering wheel with his jaw shot off, unable to help her. The siren was the high-pitched cry of some sad, wild demon coming to take away bullet-riddled bodies or the grim victims of automobile wrecks, he thought. And he thought again of his wife, Pauline.

Crumpled in the seat of the car, with blood now escaping through his fingers and the smell of gasoline and motor oil so strong he could taste it, Pusser waited, hearing the siren grow louder and louder.

Soon there was noise—people moving outside the car, voices in the night, a wrecker backing behind him, a cable unwinding. A red light, blinking like a neon sign flickered over the car. The voices were everywhere.

"Lucky he ain't dead."

"That car sure is totaled."

"By God, now tell me Pusser don't lead a charmed life."

Buford heard the scrape of metal being pulled apart and felt the pressure being taken off his body. Finally, pulled free of the wreckage, he was placed on a stretcher and laid inside a Shackleford Funeral Home ambulance. The demon, he said to himself, as he felt the rear wheels of the ambulance spin in the mud before they caught, and the vehicle jumped onto the highway, heading toward McNairy County Memorial Hospital in Selmer.

Pusser's family physician, Dr. Harry Peeler, a slender man in his mid-forties, was waiting as the sheriff was wheeled into the emergency room of the hospital. He quickly examined Pusser, then told Glen Dancer, the ambulance driver, to get ready for a trip to Memphis.

"I'm sending him to the Baptist Hospital. He's lost a lot of blood, and his left eye is really messed up," Peeler said quickly, shaking his head.

"Get him in the ambulance, Glen, while I get my coat. I'm going with you—along with an orderly."

Seconds later, Peeler climbed inside the ambulance and took a seat on a small fold-down chair next to the stretcher.

"Take it easy, Buford. Everything's going to be all right," the doctor said, forcing a smile as he checked the tube running into Pusser's arm.

Selmer's street lights glittered on the ambulance windows and cast bluish flecks across the solemn faces inside the vehicle as it sped west through town to State Highway 57. The ambulance left the city limits and careened toward Pocahontas, Saulsbury, Grand Junction, LaGrange, Moscow, Collierville, Germantown and Memphis.

Peeler checked Pusser's pulse from time to time but said nothing.

Buford stared at the low ceiling, listening to the whine of the siren, muffled as if he were in a cocoon. This is too familiar, he thought, and winced, aching for Pauline, for peace, for his life.

Dancer cut the siren, and Pusser felt nothing but the slight tremble of the speeding ambulance—and the pain. His thoughts now came in spurts, making him dizzy. His head throbbed with remembering. One moment, the round, chubby face of little Dwana, his daughter, was so close he tried to reach out and touch it—but couldn't—his heart yearning for the little girl who in only eight short years of life had lost so much; the next moment he saw the stunned, blank face of Louise Hathcock the night he had shot her to death. Her face and that of Charles Hamilton, the two people he had killed, were never very far away from him.

Then he remembered this morning, October 4, 1969, and smiled in spite of himself. They wanted to make a movie about his life, he thought, well, here's another chapter—and how would this one end?

His mind darted over everything that had happened to him, remembering in bits and snatches—his disappointing military career, the wreck right after he had been discharged, the hitchhiker, the moonshiners, the nineteen-year-old murderer who had sawed his way out of the county jail and stolen his parents' car. Buford remembered the automobile chase and the shot he had had to fire, the bullet paralyzing the boy. He thought of some of the people he had tried to help. From a few of them his reward had been a knife in the stomach or a bullet hole.

And now, death was once again reaching out for him. Lying on the stretcher, he pulled his thoughts back to the present. He heard a strange hissing sound

coming from the engine of the ambulance. Then, a
shrill noise blared out as clouds of steam spewed from
under the hood of the vehicle. The ambulance was
leaving the Collierville city limits. Dancer applied the
brakes, and Pusser felt his weight shift to one side as
the ambulance made a U-turn and headed back toward
Collierville.

Dr. Peeler shoved open the sliding window behind
Dancer.

"What's wrong, Glen?"

"This damned ambulance is hotter than hell and the
radiator is boiling like a tea kettle. I'm going back
to that service station we just passed and get some
water."

Pusser tried to raise himself up from the stretcher
with his elbows.

"Lie down, now, Buford, and take it easy. We'll
get some water and be on our way again in a minute
or two," Peeler said, gently placing his hands on
Pusser's shoulders.

Dancer braked the Cadillac ambulance in the driveway of a service station and hopped out.

"Put some water in this thing before it burns up.
And hurry. I'm on my way to the Baptist Hospital
with a man who's been in a bad smashup," Dancer
said, jerking open the hood.

The station attendant quickly brought a water hose,
then held it to one side, letting water spill down the
driveway as he peered at the engine.

"It ain't gonna do no good to put water in this

radiator, mister, because it won't stay. The water pump is shot and I ain't got one, either."

"Damn. This son of a bitch will burn slam up before I get to Memphis. What's the name of the funeral home here? I'll have to call another ambulance."

"Brantley-Hutton is the only funeral home in Collierville," the attendant answered. "Come on, you can use the phone in the office to call them."

Dancer made the telephone call, then returned to the disabled ambulance.

"The water pump went out. I called another ambulance. Should be here any second."

"I sure hope so," Peeler said. "We've got to get Buford to the hospital, and fast."

"Ain't this hell?" Pusser mumbled. "Can't even get to the hospital without the damned ambulance breaking down."

"Don't talk, Buford. Everything's going to be fine," the doctor said, pressing down on the strip of tape that held the transfusing needle in place on Pusser's arm.

Lying there on the stretcher, Buford wondered if everything really was going to be all right—if his streak of bad luck would ever end. At that moment it seemed that his life had been a stacked deck from the start.

After what seemed like an hour, the Brantley-Hutton ambulance arrived. And then the nightmare was moving again.

"We've lost a lot of time," Dr. Peeler told the new driver, "so get us there as fast as you can."

"Yes, sir."

The siren echoed through the streets of Germantown as the ambulance streaked toward the city limits of Memphis. Highway 57 blended into U. S. 72 and the traffic became heavier. The driver seldom touched his brakes as he wove his way through the cluster of morning motorists toward Union Avenue and the Baptist Hospital. Somewhere a horn tooted, air brakes hissed noisily, and gears ground angrily as a city bus moved through town. Then the ambulance stopped.

The back door swung open and Pusser's dark brown eyes squinted against the intruding daylight. Sounds of garbage cans being emptied, the whine of tires on the streets, people chattering—all echoed in unison. Memphis was awakening.

But for Buford Pusser, sleep still waited somewhere beyond the antiseptic walls of the emergency room. Visions of his youth, misty and unclear, came into his mind and left again. And at last he slept.

CHAPTER II

"I Don't Want to Go to School"

It was December 12, 1937 in Finger, Tennessee. Daisy Garner, a small woman in her early thirties, stood beside the bed where Helen Pusser had just given birth to her third child. Outside, the temperature was well below zero, and funnels of dry snow swirled across the yard and whipped the front of the three-room frame house. Inside, it was warm—almost too warm, Daisy thought, staring into the fireplace where flames licked noisily at two huge logs.

She turned and studied Helen's face, tired but calm, after the ordeal. Where on earth is the doctor, she thought. It seemed forever since Carl had burst into the house to ask her to stay with Helen while he walked to the closest telephone to call the doctor. What a night for this to happen.

*   *   *

Carl Pusser, a big man with muscles as hard as marble, plodded through knee-deep snow. He had made the five-mile trip to the Bowers' house without too much trouble. Thank God they'd been home, so he could phone Doc Tucker. The miracle was that the doctor had been home. For a second, Carl forgot how tired he was and wondered if Tucker had made it to Helen in time.

"I've got to hurry," he mumbled.

Straight ahead he saw the outline of the Plunk farm. If he could borrow a car, he could get back to Helen in a matter of minutes. Everyone was sound asleep, he realized, as he walked up the snowy path that twisted through the back yard, but there was another miracle—Plunk's old Ford was parked right beside the back porch. Now if the damned thing would just start, which he doubted, most of his worries would be over.

The first problem was the car door—frozen shut. He yanked at it until the sweat rolled down his face and froze. Finally, the door came loose and so suddenly that he lost his footing and sat down hard in the drifting snow. He got up, fumbled in his shirt pocket and found one kitchen match which he cautiously struck on the tin dashboard. In the brief and sputtering light, he saw the key dangling from the ignition.

The cold leather seat creaked as he slid into the car. He sat, peering through the windshield into the darkness, almost afraid to turn the key. Hell, he thought, if it won't start, it won't start—but I've got to try. He turned on the ignition and pushed the starter. There was no sound but a low growl. "Come on, dammit," he grumbled under his breath. After three more tries and much pumping, the engine suddenly came alive. Sounds like a tractor that hasn't been used in six months, he thought, but at least it started, and he leaned back in the seat with a sigh of relief.

*   *   *

Dr. N. A. Tucker, a husky man with thick, dark brown hair, flung open the door of the Pusser house like a sheriff armed with a search warrant.

Daisy, gently rocking the latest Pusser addition in her arms, looked up in fright.

"Well, I see Mother Nature beat me here," Tucker said. He laughed, tossing his well-worn medical bag on the foot of the bed while he got out of his overcoat.

When Daisy was finally able to catch her breath, she said, "You scared the living daylights out of me."

"Sorry," he said, "but I was afraid I wouldn't make it in time—and I didn't."

He grinned, picked up his bag and quickly examined Mrs. Pusser and the baby.

"Both of them seem to be in fine shape. I'd better be careful, Daisy, or you'll take my job away from me," he joked, taking a needle from his bag and giving Helen Pusser a sedative.

Daisy laughed weakly.

"I don't think you need to worry about that," she

said. "I sure wouldn't want to have to do that job very often."

"Nothing to it," the doctor said, sidestepping a clutter of damp wash cloths, bloodstained towels and pans of warm water on the bare wooden floor. "Carl not back yet?"

"No, and I'm a little worried. I wish he'd get here. Helen'll be asking about him before much longer." Daisy glanced at the bed, where Helen was half-buried in a sagging feather mattress, her thin body barely visible.

"Don't worry about Carl—that big strapping son-of-a-gun will make it all right. Baby got a name yet?"

"Buford Hayse," she said. "Helen said if it was a boy, that was what she wanted him named."

"Buford Hayse Pusser," the doctor said. "That sounds like a good name—sure won't be hard to remember."

"What's that?" Daisy turned. "Must be Carl."

The door flew open and Carl Pusser burst into the room.

"Is Helen all right, Doc?"

"Yep, she's doing fine and so is the youngster."

Carl glanced at his sleeping wife, then took the baby from Daisy, pulling back the faded blue blanket to see young Buford's face.

"Boy, he's a jim dandy, ain't he? He's nearly big enough right now to hold a mule in a cotton row."

Tucker grinned. "Yeah, Carl—almost. He's a big

fellow all right. I weighed him on the portable scales—
over nine pounds."

Carl handed the baby back to Daisy.

"He doesn't know it, but I went through hell for
him tonight," Carl said. "I had to walk five miles to
call you, then steal a car to get back here."

"Whose car did you borrow?" Tucker asked.

"Prince Plunk's Ford, and I was damned lucky to
find the keys in it. I was even luckier that it'd start. No
telling how long it had been sitting there. I'll drive it
over there after a while and he can bring me home."
Tucker sighed. "All of a sudden I'm dead tired," he
said. "Guess I'll get on home. That's a fine boy you've
got there, Carl, and Helen's doing all right, too. Guess
she's a bit tired, though." He got up, took another
brief look at Helen, and picked up his medical bag.
"Didn't leave anything, did I?" He looked quickly
around the room and moved toward the door.

"Thanks a lot for coming out tonight, Doc. For
the time being, you'll just have to settle for thanks.
With cotton selling so bad, it's been hard as hell
making ends meet. It's been a tough year for farmers."
Carl smiled.

"It ain't been too good for doctors, either. I'll check
on Helen and the boy again tomorrow. Good night."

" 'Night, Doc, and thanks again."

Carl watched the doctor get into his car, and then
closed the door.

"Daisy," he said, "it's been a hell of a night, ain't

it?" Daisy, holding Buford, was sound asleep in the rocking chair.

*   *   *

Although it was 1937, West Tennessee was still feeling the pinch of the depression. There were still block-long lines at the government commodity stations; cotton was selling for five cents a pound, and regular jobs were few and far between.

Like most other West Tennessee families, the Pussers were struggling for survival. There was no money for staples, or seed, or clothing. Bills went unpaid. The only thing that wasn't scarce was food. Helen Pusser spent the summer canning everything from vegetables to preserves, and there were always plenty of potatoes, eggs, meat and lard. Sugar, flour, coffee and salt were not plentiful, however.

Carl tried to persuade himself that things were bound to get better, but he found it hard to accept his own philosophy.

Roosevelt, who had been elected to a second term in 1936, was trying to remedy the economic problems through large expenditures of public money and the creation of jobs. But in 1937, Roosevelt's plan had not been very effective in West Tennessee. There was still a great deal of unemployment and Carl, a dyed-in-the-wool Republican, took some pleasure in telling everyone that the Democrats hadn't done any better than the Republicans had.

"We'd have had a depression no matter who was in the White House," he said often. "It was just one of those things."

Times were bad, but Carl was among the fortunate. When he wasn't farming he had a job at Albert Plunk's sawmill. He worked sixteen hours a day, six days a week, and the pay was fifty cents a day. On Sundays, he was a self-made barber. On a typical weekend he would have thirty or thirty-five customers at five cents a head.

Shortly after Buford was born, however, Carl thought about giving up the barbering. He was worn out with the long hours at the sawmill and the chores at home. But the thought of the approaching Christmas season changed his mind. There would have to be *some* kind of Christmas for Helen and the kids, even though times were hard. Buford, of course, would be no problem. He was too little to know what Christmas was all about, but the older children would be disappointed. He would need every dime he could earn, so he kept plodding through the days, tired, more asleep than awake most of the time.

Christmas came and went, with the apples, oranges, candy, Helen's cakes and pies, and the annual supply of whiskey. Although Carl drank very little, every Christmas he and some of his neighbors went together and ordered gallon jugs from a distillery in Cairo, Illinois. One man was designated to make the two-hundred mile trip to bring back the whiskey. The gaiety of the season dispersed the gloom for a little while, but then it was back to the business of trying to make a living.

Winter faded gradually, and the valley shook with the hum of logs passing through the sawmill. Spring was coming—crop time—but for Carl, who had neither the seed for spring planting nor the money to buy any, it was a period of constant worry.

One day he slammed the corncrib door shut and stalked toward the house. Trapped again, he thought, just like some damned varmint. He went into the house, brushed roughly past Helen, and flung himself into a kitchen chair.

"It's pretty damned bad when a man works day and night and still doesn't have enough money to buy seed," he complained.

Helen opened the oven door and inspected a pan of corn bread.

"Carl, all that cuss'n and yell'n ain't gonna help matters any. The best thing to do is go to Selmer and borrow some money from the Seed and Loan Office. Why don't you just face it?"

Carl, still sulking in the chair, took a bag of tobacco from the pocket of his worn overalls, shook some into a cigarette paper, jerked the sack strings closed with his teeth and crammed the sack back into his pocket.

"Borrow, borrow! That's all a poor man does all his damned life," he muttered. "Everything a poor son of a bitch makes belongs to some other bastard before he even gets his own hands on it." He licked the rolled cigarette, put it in his mouth, and lit it.

"Like I said, Carl, that language ain't gonna buy any seed."

In spite of the argument with his wife, Carl decided that there was nothing to do but follow her advice. He went to Selmer the next day and borrowed seventy-five dollars from the Seed and Loan Office, agreeing to buy fertilizer to plant the crops. Although this was part of the government requirement, Carl didn't agree with it and didn't mince any words in saying so.

It was the same damned thing year after year, Carl thought—borrowing money, hunting ginseng (which sold for thirty dollars a pound when you could find that much), plowing with a pair of mules, working at the sawmill, and being a weekend barber. He watched Buford outgrow his baby clothes and wondered if he would have to travel the same road. He worried about Buford's strong attachment to his mother. He'd have to outgrow that if he was ever going to get anywhere.

Buford Pusser was a quiet, timid boy who stayed close to Helen's side day in and day out. Sometimes when she turned too quickly, she stepped on him. When that happened, she would reprimand him for not playing with the other youngsters in the neighborhood, but Buford didn't understand his mother's viewpoint. He couldn't understand her explanation of why he should go to school, either.

Helen Pusser, a patient woman, tried to convince

Buford Pusser at age seven.

Buford that getting an education was important. "I want you to have more than I did," she would say, but her words had no effect on him.

"Please, Mommy, I don't want to go to school," Buford begged, over and over, hanging on to his mother's dress. "I want to stay home with you."

Helen didn't go into the subject again until September 1942, the year that Buford was five.

"Listen, son, you have to go to school. When you get older, you'll be glad I made you go—do you hear me?" she argued, frowning in desperation. She dipped her hands into a pan of water, patted her son's hair and combed back the unruly locks. Buford continued to protest. "I don't want to go to school," he sobbed. "I don't want to go to school till I'm forty years old."

Helen turned her head away from her son and laughed silently. She understood his feeling for her and, in part, blamed herself for letting him become so attached. She had enjoyed his strong affection. The other children were older and growing more independent of her, but Buford was still a baby.

"Buford, you've got to go to school whether you like it or not. It's the law. They can put your father and me in jail if we don't make you go. Besides, you'll like school once you go and meet all the other kids and play games with them. You'll see."

Unfortunately, however, things did not turn out as Helen had predicted. Once Buford was finally pushed out of the house and away from the protection of his mother, he found a hostile world among the other children at Finger School. Because he was shy, he was the object of laughter. The older boys teased him until he wanted to fight back somehow, but he just couldn't do it, and this only made the teasing louder and more frequent. Every morning he went through the same arguments with his mother. He begged her to let him stay home, and when she made him go to school, he cried.

Helen didn't tell Carl about the problem, for fear that he would take a switch to the boy. Carl almost always lost his temper when he punished the children, and she was afraid he would really lose it now. He had never said much about it, but she felt that he blamed her for Buford's attitude.

She tolerated Buford's tantrums for two months, but the strain finally became too much and she made a bargain with him. He could stay out of school until he was six years old; then he would have to go—regardless.

Helen Pusser kept her part of the bargain, and two months later when Buford reached his sixth birthday, she took him to school once again. Since she thought it might be better for him to enter a new school where he wouldn't be haunted by unpleasant memories, she enrolled him in the Leapwood School.

His new teacher, Mrs. Cory Hare, seemed to have a way with him, and to Helen's surprise, Buford began to adjust. However, his adjustment came too late. Because he was several weeks behind the other first graders in studies, he was not promoted to the second grade at the end of the school year. The boy was disappointed and resentful, Helen thought. He *had* tried and it was going to take all summer to get him over that.

During the summer, Buford whiled away the days fishing in a creek on the Pusser farm with a cane pole he had made himself. He usually caught a few Sun Perch, and for a little while he was able to keep his mind off school. He wished that the summer would never end.

Late in August, Buford put aside his fishing pole and helped the family gather the peanut crop. It was the first time he had been asked to help with the chores, and he was proud. Maybe he could do something to help after all.

He never forgot his first day in the peanut patch. The sun illuminated the sky with an unreal intensity and splashed heat waves over the red clay. Buford wiped sweat from his forehead with the back of his hand and tugged at a peanut vine behind Molly Harris, his grandmother. She pulled a cluster of peanuts from the ground, then spat a stream of snuff into the loose dirt. Buford watched her with mounting inquisitiveness. His grandmother had dipped snuff and his grandfather, Bliss Harris, had chewed tobacco ever since he could remember. Now, in the hot sun, pulling on the peanut plants, sweating as his parents and grandparents had for years, he wanted to try some snuff.

"Give me some snuff, Grandma," Buford demanded. His mother had always told him that dipping and chewing were nasty habits, but if Grandma and Grandpa did, he couldn't see that there was anything wrong with either one.

"You're too little," she said.

"No, I'm not—I'm in the first grade, and I'm big enough."

"I said no, Buford."

Carl, pulling peanuts nearby, broke into the conversation.

"Go on, Molly, give him some snuff. He's as stubborn as a young jackass. He won't be satisfied until he finds out for himself that he's not near as big as he thinks he is."

Helen Pusser objected, but it did no good. Carl took a small can of snuff from Mrs. Harris, pulled out Buford's lower lip, and filled it full of finely ground tobacco. Buford licked some of the snuff into his mouth, then swallowed it. He coughed and tried to "hawk" it up but couldn't. His eyes filled with tears, and the ground spun like a merry-go-round. He vomited, and vomited, and finally passed out. Carl scooped him up in his arms and carried him to the house. Buford had the dry heaves for three days, and from that day on, tobacco in any form made him sick.

*   *   *

In September, Buford again entered the first grade at Leapwood, and after a few weeks, he even seemed to enjoy going to school. Even though he was big for his six years, he still let other boys push him around, but he was quick to defend a smaller boy who was being picked on. A school day seldom passed without Buford's coming home with cuts and bruises, usually the result of his encounters with school bullies. This infuriated Carl Pusser.

"Why in hell don't you knock the piss out of those little bastards when they mess with you?" his father scolded. "Don't let them shove you around. The more you take, the more they'll dish out. Beat their asses once and they'll leave you alone." Helen whirled from the stove in anger.

"Carl, that isn't any way to talk to your son—using all that filthy talk—that's a shame and a disgrace!"

"Oh, yeah," Carl snapped. "Let him grow up to be a sissy. First thing you know, he'll be squatting to take a piss."

Carl stormed out of the house.

His stern words had no effect on Buford, however. He continued to let himself be bullied and his five years at Leapwood did little to change that.

* * *

In 1948, Mrs. Pusser enrolled Buford in the sixth grade at the Adamsville Elementary School. He rode the school bus to Adamsville, but would not ride the bus to special school functions. Still timid and shy at the age of eleven, he was afraid he would get lost if he rode the bus anywhere except to school and back.

For the next two years, Buford stayed in his mother's shadow, but in 1950, to Carl's delight, he hired out for his first job. Charlie Duren, owner of a general store in Adamsville, hired Buford to mow the lawn, trim hedges around his house, and plow and plant his garden. Buford took pride in all of the work, but he enjoyed the garden chores the most. He made an extra effort to lay down straight rows when he was planting, and Duren often told Buford that the rows were the straightest he had ever seen. The more Duren complimented him, the harder Buford worked. There was something different about working for someone else, he thought. He worked hard at home, but that was expected of him. It was not like a real job.

In 1951, Carl Pusser decided it was time to give up trying to support the family from his barely productive farm. He had to find a regular job. John, Buford's older brother, had already dropped out of school and was working. After a few days of job hunting, Carl found employment with a construction cleanup crew in Columbia, Tennessee.

Carl's leaving left Buford and Helen with the responsibility of making a crop, but Buford, although only thirteen years old, readily accepted the challenge.

He spent hours driving the old Farmall tractor, plowing the fields, and cultivating the cotton and corn rows. When he wasn't plowing, hoeing, or thinning cotton, he helped his mother work the truck garden. He gave the vegetables special attention, since the food supply for another year depended on that garden.

By mid-summer, however, the lack of rain threatened to destroy all that they had worked for. In the fields, the corn hardened too fast and the silks turned brown too quickly.

The faded green leaves were heavy with dust and stirred lazily in an occasional slight breeze. Tiny green-winged bugs buzzed among the scrawny cotton stalks, and lizards scampered over the parched ground, along the dry, hard-packed rows.

When the crops had been planted, Buford began to spend most of his time cleaning up around the farm. He raked and burned the dead tree limbs and other debris which had collected during the winter.

One July evening, Helen Pusser leaned against a rail fence near the barn and a smile passed over her worried face as she watched smoke from burning rubbish hover close to the ground.

"It's finally going to rain, Buford," she said. "The Lord is going to save our crops."

"How do you know, Mom?"

"Because, when smoke hovers near the ground, it's a sure sign of rain."

Coincidence or not, showers fell most of the next day, giving new life to the fields of dying crops. Although the crops were not the best ones ever raised on the Pusser farm, they were good enough to keep the creditors happy and to put food on the table for another year.

When the harvest chores were finished, Buford and his mother decided one Saturday afternoon to attend a horse show in Adamsville and get away from the daily grind on the farm.

Buford had learned to drive an old Hudson that his father had left at home for the lack of gasoline money, and he persuaded his mother to let him drive to the horse show.

When the Adamsville city limits sign came into

view, he had the Hudson running well over seventy.

"Slow this car down, Buford," Helen Pusser said sharply. "You're going to kill both of us." She had been complaining about her son's fast driving ever since they had left home.

Buford slowed the car to fifty.

"You're still driving too fast. Now slow down!"

The speedometer needle dropped to the forty mark.

"If you don't slow down, I'm going to tell your father, and you know what that will mean."

Buford braked the car until the speedometer read five miles per hour.

"Do you think this is slow enough?" he asked sarcastically, "or should I just park?"

"Don't get smart, Buford, or you won't ever drive this car again. I'll see to that—hear?" she warned.

Realizing that he was in danger of losing his short-lived driving privilege, young Pusser hastily apologized to his mother for his sharp words and promised to drive more slowly in the future.

*   *   *

The summer of 1951 had been a testing ground for Buford Pusser. He had found that he could successfully do his father's work on the farm and had proved to himself that he could shoulder a man's responsibility.

In the fall, Buford took up his eighth grade studies

at Adamsville Elementary and worked after school and on Saturdays at Duren's store. His responsibilities included the loading and delivering of feed and supplies to farmers.

Early in 1952, Carl Pusser came home from Columbia for a visit. He had worked hard on his job and had been rewarded with a promotion to foreman.

During his brief stay, the family moved from the farm at Finger to a small frame house in Adamsville. Only a few days after they were settled in the new house, Carl had orders from his company officials to join the crew in Columbus, Mississippi, and prepare to work in Mississippi and Louisiana, where the company had commitments to lay pipelines. Helen and Buford said good-bye to Carl, and at the same time, said farewell to planting crops, worrying about rain, and keeping tabs on the cotton market.

*   *   *

Buford managed to maintain average grades in school, and in the spring he graduated from Adamsville Elementary. Immediately following his graduation, he went to work full-time at Duren's store. He worked hard, and his cotton shirt, when he wore one, was always soaked with sweat, his face and arms, and khaki trousers and plow shoes holding dust from the heavy sacks of feed.

Buford liked his work, and occasionally thought

SCHOOL DAYS 1953-54
ADAMSVILLE HIGH

Buford Pusser in high school football uniform.

about quitting school and working year-round for Duren, but he knew he would stir up a hornet's nest at the Pusser home if he ever even mentioned the idea to his mother. Consequently, he prepared for his first year at Adamsville High, where he was to find, for the first time, an interest in athletics.

*   *   *

Inside the red brick school building it was quiet and cool; the students had all gone home, and only the sound of the janitor's wide broom sweeping over the scarred, hardwood floors broke the stillness.

Across the road, on the Carlie Hughes Memorial Field, it was neither quiet nor cool. The smack of shoulder pads, the dull thud of toe meeting pigskin, and the grunts and groans of sweating players marked the afternoon football practice.

Coach Max Hile, a short, heavyset man, built like a Green Bay Packer lineman, stood in the end zone with his hands on his hips, watching the inexperienced freshmen hopefuls mingling with his returning lettermen in mock game drills.

"Hey!" he shouted, then said more softly to one of the student managers, "What's that big kid's name? Yeah, Pusser. Hey, Pusser! Get your head down. Keep it down and hit 'em hard!"

Although Hile had seen Pusser in action only briefly, he was impressed with the boy's athletic ability.

After the workout, Hile walked among the players, as they changed clothes in the gymnasium. He stopped beside Buford, who was grinning at the antics of one of his teammates.

"Pusser."

Buford snapped to attention.

"Yessir."

"How much do you weigh?"

"Hundred seventy pounds."

"That's about what I figured. How old are you?"

"I'll be fifteen in December."

The coach smiled. He had found his fullback, and Buford Pusser had found the way to a new life.

Buford liked the rough physical contact of football and the close companionship offered by the other players on the team. Although he was still somewhat of a loner, more inclined to listen than to talk, now he belonged. He was part of a team and it was a good feeling.

He was a handsome youth with a boyish grin, popular with the girls and respected by the boys at Adamsville High.

The hard-charging Pusser kept local fans talking about his fakes and broken field running, and when his first season on the high school football field was over, no one, especially Cardinal opponents, doubted his ability to play football. When the basketball season began, Coach T. E. Chism had a place for him on the Redbird basketball team.

He was a good shot, hitting the basket for several points in every game. His ability inspired a great deal of discussion about his athletic talents. Some Cardinal boosters said Pusser performed even better on a hardwood floor than he did on the football field. Others maintained the opposite.

In the spring, Buford tried his hand at baseball, but

his poor hitting kept him on the bench most of the season, and he saw very little action on the diamond during his entire high school athletic career. He loved football and basketball and played his heart out for the Adamsville teams, at the same time struggling to maintain the passing grades necessary to continue playing.

Athletics had made the first two years of high school more tolerable for Buford, but early in his junior year he ran into trouble with his studies. Failing two subjects, history and biology, he dropped out of school after a few weeks and went to Wynnewood, Oklahoma, a small town between Ardmore and Norman, where he got a job working on a pipeline. Helen, disappointed as she was, reluctantly gave him permission to go.

Pusser wrote his mother often and received many letters from her. He wrote her about his job, the rolling hills of Oklahoma, and the Creek Indians. He seemed to be especially intrigued with the Indians and sent home snapshots of himself taken with several Indian youths. Buford's letters indicated that he was well pleased with his new life, but Helen Pusser was neither content nor happy. She wanted her youngest son to come home and finish high school, and in each letter she pleaded with him to quit his job on the pipeline and pack his suitcase. Buford refused to give in to his mother's urgings, but he did try to console her with his letters.

"I like my job and I'm making good money," he wrote. "I'm saving most of what I earn and someday

Buford with Indian boy in Wynnewood, Oklahoma.

I'll be able to buy the things we have always wanted but never had the money for. Please be patient, and remember that I love you very much."

Helen Pusser was a patient woman, but she was also an iron-willed one. While Buford was away, she borrowed some history and biology textbooks from the school library and studied so she would be able to tutor him.

When Buford found out what his mother was doing, he could no longer ignore her pleadings to come home. He left the pipeline job which he had held for six weeks, went back to Adamsville, and reentered the eleventh grade. With his mother's help, he managed to make up his lost time and failing grades. He studied diligently after returning to his junior class, determined to repay his mother for all she had done to get him back in school.

For this reason, he turned down many invitations from his school friends to accompany them to the state-line joints. Deep down, he wanted to go, and his curiosity grew as he listened to the conversations of boys who had been—"Boy, that White Iris is something, Buford. Sure wish you'd go with us some night."

He continued to spend every night studying, but eventually a strange hunger for excitement and action weakened him. One December evening, just before his seventeenth birthday, he agreed to go with two of his friends, telling his mother they were going to ride around for a while.

Buford had grown up hearing about the brawls, gambling, drinking and easy women on the strip. He knew that in the early forties young men from the CCC Camp at Selmer had found excitement and, more often, trouble in the cheap joints less than twenty miles away. Now, in 1954, new life had flowed into the strip with the closing of whorehouses and casinos in Phenix City, Alabama.

It was in 1954 that Albert Patterson had campaigned for state attorney general on a pledge to clean up the crime and corruption in the Alabama border town. He succeeded, but not as attorney general. The cleanup came after he had been shot in an ambush-slaying that finally aroused the public, brought in the National Guard, and sent the underworld characters scurrying for cover. Some of them went to jail. Others merely shifted their operations to the Tennessee-Mississippi state line.

Buford, like other people who had heard about the famous strip, wanted to see it firsthand. With his friends, he went to the White Iris Club, which sat amidst a scenic landscape just inside the Tennessee line. The run-down structure looked as out of place in the setting as a shack on the White House lawn. The outside needed painting, and countless streams of rain water from the roof had stained the once-white sides a dirty yellow.

The twangy voice of Webb Pierce penetrated the still air outside the club as Pusser and the two other high school boys piled out of an old car. The three boys stood for a moment and listened to the loud music vibrating from the juke box.

> *There stands the glass*
> *That will hide all my fears,*
> *That will drown all my tears,*
> *Brother, I'm on my way. . . .*

Clouds of thick, blue smoke drifted out the door

as Buford and his two friends entered the dimly lit lounge. They worked their way through the crowd, brushing past the half-drunk couples swaying on the dance floor, and found an empty table in a back corner of the room. Loud, drunken shouts rose above the sad country music and, during the brief lull between record changes, the steady clatter of dice mingled with the tinkling of ice cubes.

Pusser and his buddies, half-embarrassed, sat at the table, trying to hide their innocence behind beaded bottles of beer. They had bought the beer without any questions being asked about their age.

What are we doing here? Buford thought, beginning to wish they hadn't come. He felt nervous, not knowing why exactly, but afraid that something terrible might happen.

Suddenly, as loud shouts erupted near a back room, a murmur ran through the crowd.

"I wonder what's going on over there?" Pusser asked, looking across the room to see a sailor arguing with a slender, red-faced man.

"There ain't much tell'n," quipped one of the boys at the table. "Anything is liable to happen in this joint."

Louise Hathcock, a short, stocky brunette who managed the place, hurried from behind the bar armed with a claw-hammer.

"What's going on here?" she yelled.

"This bastard says he got cheated," sneered the red-faced man, who was a club employee.

"Cheated, hell," Louise Hathcock snapped. "I'll teach this son of a bitch a lesson he won't forget.

"What's the idea of coming in here and accusing us of stealing your money, you little sawed-off bastard? Talk like that around here will get your dick knocked in the dirt," she threatened.

Then, without warning, she swung the hammer and it struck a crunching blow against the sailor's head. He stumbled backward and then fell to the floor.

"Get up, you son of a bitch, get up!" Louise screamed.

The sailor, blood streaming from a gash on his head, struggled to his knees and started crawling toward the door. Louise Hathcock ran after him and swung the hammer again and again, pounding his head with sickening thuds.

"Let's get out of here," Buford ordered his two friends. He had never felt so sick.

The boys worked their way toward the door, glancing through the cluster of people to see the bleeding sailor, lying still in a pool of blood on the floor.

Before they could get to the door, it opened and a deputy sheriff strolled in. He took one last draw from a cigar stub, ground it into the floor with his shoe, and looked at the fallen sailor.

"What in the world happened, Louise?" he asked. Buford could see the beginning of a smirk on the deputy's face.

"The bastard just died of a heart attack," she answered, as nervous laughter rippled through the crowd.

"All right, Louise, if you say so." He grinned. "Get me a drink while I call an ambulance."

Buford and his two friends slipped out the door, relieved to be out of the smoke and the heat and the smell. The air was cool and refreshing.

"She killed that sailor!" Buford said. "She beat him to death with a hammer and that damn deputy didn't do a thing about it!"

He could hardly believe that it had actually happened.

"You could tell that her and the deputy were in cahoots," one of the boys said. "Didn't you hear him order a drink? He's probably getting a payoff besides."

"Yeah, it's disgusting," Buford said. "Nobody's safe with that kind of thing going on."

He had just gotten his first look at Louise Hathcock in action and his first taste of state-line activities. In later years their paths would cross again, but Buford would be a long time forgetting his first visit to the White Iris.

*   *   *

With the help of his mother, Buford squeezed through the eleventh grade and again worked at the Duren store that summer. During his senior year in high school, he maintained interest in his studies and had little difficulty in the classroom.

In the meantime, his exploits on the football field

attracted talent scouts from a number of colleges. Although he had missed a season the previous year when he had been in Oklahoma, the time lost was not evident when he was in the game.

In basketball, he led the Adamsville team with a 27-point average and helped the Cardinals defeat such opponents as Scotts Hill, Jackson, Lexington, Savannah, Sardis, Selmer, Henderson and Middleton to capture the district title.

The team also participated in the regional tournament at Memphis.

For Coach T. E. Chism, a tall, rail-thin man with a boyish smile, a Redbird victory in the tournament was riding on Buford Pusser. He was counting heavily on Pusser's 27-point per game average to help Adamsville bring home the gold championship trophy from Memphis and, later, one from the state tournament.

As Buford led the Cardinals to an easy victory over Lexington East in the opening game, Chism's hopes rose, but they proved to be short-lived.

Before the next night's game against Memphis East, Pusser had come down with the mumps.

In spite of his feverish condition, however, Buford insisted on dressing for the game. After talking to Dr. Glen Abernathy, the team physician, Chism decided to let Buford sit on the bench, but the doctor advised the coach not to use him in the game unless the team got into a do-or-die situation.

The Redbirds held a comfortable lead over Memphis East until the third quarter. Then, Memphis began to move, and the scoreboard blinked one-sidedly as the point margin narrowed. Chism paced back and forth in front of the Cardinal bench nervously fingering his belt buckle. When the buzzer ended the third period, Adamsville clung to a slim three-point lead.

"Come here, Buford," Chism commanded in a sharper-than-usual tone of voice.

Pusser sprang to his feet.

"Go in there and guard that big tall boy close. He's killing us with all those long shots," Chism said, hitting Pusser on the rear as he trotted onto the floor with the other players.

With a shot in the arm from Pusser, Adamsville quickly increased its lead in the fourth quarter and coasted to an easy victory.

The following night Buford was so much worse that Dr. Abernathy refused to allow him to dress for the game with Jackson. As a result, the Adamsville team lost, while Buford sat on the bench nursing his swollen glands. Having the mumps any time would be bad enough, he thought, but having them tonight just wasn't fair.

In the spring of 1956 Buford Pusser graduated from Adamsville High School. When he received his diploma, Helen knew that she must be the happiest person in the auditorium. Her patience and determination had finally paid off.

Shortly after graduation, Buford received several offers of football scholarships, the most tempting one

Buford's high school graduation photograph.

being from Florida State University. There were many times when he seriously considered signing.

In the privacy of his room, he often admired the seven letters he had received, three in football and four in basketball. When he looked at the large red "A" 's, he dreamed of headlines on the sports pages telling the world about the McNairy County fullback who was shattering college records.

Headlines were indeed in store for Buford, but they wouldn't come from his hard-charging maneuvers on a football field.

CHAPTER III

"I'm Going to Join the Marines"

It was that time of year when the earth seemed to turn slower and the sound of living had idled to a low murmur.

The excitement of spring was gone, the smells of freshly turned dirt and budding leaves had faded with the cry of mating birds, and the dry, lazy feel of summer gripped the days. Crops had been planted and the earth, like a pregnant woman, waited for the corn and cotton to make. The farmers had done all they could do against the grass. Now their plows were still.

It was that way in Adamsville, too. Merchants, looking through the front panes of their stores, could almost see the heat rising from the pavement. Clerks folded and refolded stacks of trousers, shirts and socks, and talked of vacations, picnics and watermelon cuttings. In the evenings, the sound of locusts was broken now and then with the screech of rubber and the whine of engines as young men wheeled through the streets, looking for ways to pass the time.

The teen-agers often gathered at a small cafe where they ate hamburgers, sipped soft drinks, and played the jukebox.

Out in front of Duren's General Store, farmers talked about the cotton crop; about how many bales per acre they thought they would make and whether the market would be up or down.

Inside, Buford stacked sacks of feed against a wall, wiped sweat off his forehead, and thought about leaving Adamsville. He wanted to see the world. His period of growing up was almost behind him and he was restless—no longer a boy and yet not quite a man— on his own and yet not quite severed from the ties of home. The streets of Adamsville were too quiet; the football field, now silent, belonged to another time. He often thought about the scholarships he had been offered and asked himself why he had turned them down. He craved excitement. He might have found it on a college football field, but it was too late to think about that now. He wanted to go places, to see and do things. He was looking for an open door to the outside world—away from Adamsville, which in his mind was becoming a trap, a cage.

It was a sign in front of the post office which finally pointed the way—the Marine Corps. He studied the pictures of the handsome young men in uniform and saw a glint of glamor and adventure in their eyes. He imagined himself in the dress blues, coming home in uniform, proud and straight. But he also had a vision of himself hugging the ground in some far-off place while bullets whizzed dangerously past him. The Marines had a reputation for being the toughest branch of the military service, and the tougher anything was, Buford thought, the better he liked it. His decision was made.

Now his only problem was to break the news to his mother without causing a scene. Since she worked at a clothing manufacturing firm in Savannah, he had only that night or the next morning to tell her. He planned to discuss the matter with her that night at supper, but he lost his nerve and decided to wait until breakfast. After all, he couldn't enlist until the next day anyway. The following morning, after breakfast, he broke the news.

"I'm going to join the Marines," he said bluntly. Somehow, there wasn't any other way to say it.

"What did you say?" Helen asked, somewhat stunned.

"I said I'm going to join the Marines. My mind is made up and nothing can change it."

Helen Pusser set her half-full coffee cup down on the table and studied it briefly. Then she started stacking the breakfast dishes, taking them to the sink without saying a word.

"Now, Mom, please try to understand. The Marines will be good for me. I'll learn a trade, and when I get out, I'll be able to get a good-paying job."

"If you wanted to learn a trade, you should have

planned to go to college this fall. That would have been much better than joining the Marines."

Buford got up, went to his mother and put his arms around her waist.

"Please, Mom. It's not the end of the world. Besides, I'll have to go to the service sooner or later, so I might as well get it over with. Anyway, I think I'd like it. I might even want to make a career of it. I've got to do something."

Buford's words touched her. She had not really thought about it before, but he was right; in a short time, the draft would probably get him. Besides, she could tell that he had already reached a final decision.

"Well," she said quietly, "I guess you're right. I hate to see you go now, but one time is about as good as another when it comes to doing something that has to be done."

The next day, Buford went alone to the recruiting office and signed up for a three-year hitch. No more feed sacks, Saturday night movies, squirrel stews, coon suppers and catfish dinners, he thought. He said goodbye to the slow-crawling streets of Adamsville, Tennessee. He was going where the action was. As the day of departure drew nearer, however, he was surprised at the sadness that touched him. He didn't say anything to his mother about it—but it *was* a big step he was taking. At odd moments he wondered if he had made the right decision, but right or wrong, he had to try it.

On August 9, 1956, a bus came to Adamsville and

picked up Buford and several other young men from the area. They first went to Jackson and then to Nashville, where they were sworn in and put on a train to Parris Island, South Carolina, for basic training. Buford's days of freedom ended when he was absorbed into the Fifth Recruit Training Battalion along with other young men from across the country. He exchanged his sport shirt and summer trousers for drab-green fatigues, then climbed into a barber's chair and got his head shaved in a "white sidewall." Days and nights ran together as he tried to adjust to the nerve-shattering reveille at 6:00 A. M. and to the gravel-voiced commands of the drill instructors.

"All right, you guys, fall out. And if you don't know what that means, you'd better find out real fast," growled a well-built drill instructor. He looked as if he hated his own mother, Buford thought.

The recruits straggled together in four crooked rows. The DI strutted out beside the first row, then looked down the long, snakelike lines.

"Ain't this a sight for sore eyes?" he sneered. "Looks like a bunch of raggy-ass bums trying to wiggle out of a bucket of shit."

He swaggered down to the next row, then suddenly turned and came back.

"Straighten this damned row up, and straighten it up fast," he yelled. "Anybody ought to have enough sense to stand in a straight line."

Pusser had his own ideas about common sense and wondered why the Marine Corps didn't obtain instruc-

Buford at Parris Island, S. C.

tors who were a little more human. Several times he wanted to say so aloud, but something told him it wouldn't be the thing to do.

The hot, clammy mornings became crowded with calisthenics, close-order drills and tiring marches. The strict discipline robbed Pusser of his self-will and ego for awhile, but it didn't strip him of his determination to be a good Marine. At night, bone-tired, and sometimes homesick, Buford would lie on his bunk and ease his weariness by telling himself that at least he had kept up with the pace. And this alone, this knowledge that he was man enough to stay in the harness, made each day a little easier to face.

Still somewhat shy and withdrawn, he seldom joined in conversation with the other recruits in the barracks; however, his lack of participation did not keep them from teasing him about his Southern background.

"Come on, Tennessee. Tell us about that high-powered moonshine whiskey you used to make and about the hillbilly gals you laid," laughed a tall, skinny, freckle-faced youth from Ohio.

Several other recruits gathered around.

"I hear you Rebels really have a ball drinking white lighting and rolling in the hay loft with those country gals," he added.

Buford grinned. Though shy, he was easygoing and tried not to pay any attention to the ribbing from his barracks mates. Some of the boys from the North were always teasing him about his Southern drawl or about customs in the South.

"Tell us the truth, now, Tennessee, does them gals down South really like it better than the gals up North?"

Buford hesitated a moment, then finally blurted, "I hate to give you the run-around, but I just don't know—I never have had a Yankee girl."

The recruits laughed, and Buford blushed in spite of himself.

The food in the mess hall was a far cry from his mother's cooking. For a while, Buford thought he would never acquire an appetite for it, but the endless training sessions soon changed his mind. Anything tasted good after awhile, he decided. The mosquitoes and sand fleas he found more difficult to accept. They flourished in the swampy, junglelike lowlands of Parris Island, where palmettoes and nut grass grew in abundance. He dreamed of the last day of basic training, when he would be able to leave the island. Almost any place would be better than this.

The drills and constant marching were finally replaced by hours on the firing range. Pusser enjoyed triggering the M-1 rifle and .45-caliber pistol, and he became a crack shot. Although Buford considered his maneuvers on the firing range to be quite successful, his supervisor thought otherwise and made numerous comments to that effect.

"Keep flat on the ground and keep your head down when you're firing from a prone position," the instructor ordered. "If you stick your head up like that in combat, you'll get it blown clean off your shoulders. Then it'll be too damned late to learn about your mistake."

Pusser, smelling of rifle oil and burnt powder,

squeezed off another shot with the M-1. The bullet zipped through the black bull's-eye on the paper target, and the supervisor made no more comments.

*   *   *

Even though it rained often, the island was soon dusty again, and a strange tightness crept into Buford's chest. Sometimes he had to fight to get his breath, but he thought the problem was probably minor and continued to go through the strenuous training exercises. It was the damned dust, he thought to himself. His condition gradually worsened, however, and he was sent to the base infirmary. After a series of examinations and tests, the military doctors discovered that Buford's trouble was asthma, and he was immediately sent to the naval hospital at Beaufort, South Carolina.

Although Marine officials seemed very much interested in his condition, Buford could get little or no information from the doctors. As the days dragged on, he was frequently visited by a Marine lieutenant who didn't seem familiar with any subject but medical discharges. Buford was depressed at the prospect of being discharged and clung to the hope that the asthma would improve and he could go on with his plans for a professional military career. That was what he really wanted to do, he had decided, and it would be a damned shame if everything blew up in his face now.

His navy doctor brought him good news one morning, but it had nothing to do with his health.

"They told me at the desk to give you this letter, Buford. It's probably from your girl friend back home."

"I haven't got any girl friend back home," Buford said.

He opened the letter while the doctor probed and thumped on his chest.

"Well, what do you know? My dad has quit his pipeline job and he's been made chief of police at Adamsville. Boy, that's sure good."

"Yeah, you're not kidding. Now if any of my friends ever get a ticket in Adamsville, I'll know who to contact," the doctor said, laughing.

"Say, Doc, how am I doing?"

"You're going to live. You've improved a lot in the past few days."

"Do you think they'll discharge me?"

"At this stage, I really don't know."

"Come on, Doc, level with me."

"Like I said, ole buddy, I really don't know at this time. Anyway, if you get out, your father will probably make you a cop. That'll be a lot better than being a Marine. You'll be giving orders then instead of taking them," the doctor said. He left the room and Buford was left alone again to wonder.

Four days later, the lieutenant, whom Pusser had come to know well, told him that the Marines planned to discharge him.

"But I don't want a discharge," Buford protested.

"I want to make a career out of the Marines. Why does everything I do turn out wrong?"

"Just take it easy now and rest," the lieutenant urged. "I'll talk to the top brass and see what I can do for you. Maybe, just maybe, something can be worked out. After all, it isn't every day that we get ahold of a man who's as dedicated to the Marines as you are." The words encouraged Buford, and he let his hopes rise higher and higher as he waited.

The lieutenant's efforts produced no results, however, and Buford suffered his first major disappointment. On November 14, 1956, the Marines handed him a medical discharge, along with a hundred dollars in cash and directions to the local bus station.

Buford was more than dejected—he was miserable. It seemed that everything he wanted to do or dreamed of doing had a way of falling through. At nineteen, I'm a complete failure, he thought.

*   *   *

Buford Pusser stared at his reflection in the window beside his seat near the front of the Greyhound bus. He had slipped on his uniform coat in preparation for his arrival in Adamsville. Using the windowpane for a mirror, he carefully smoothed down the collar of his coat, straightened his tie, and adjusted his cap.

For a moment he admired his boyish image in the greenish Marine uniform and thought of the day just three months earlier when he had dreamed of coming home dressed as he was now. He had dreamed of driving through the streets of Adamsville and around the court square in Selmer to let everyone know he was a United States Marine. Now, the bout with asthma had shattered his dreams and in less than twenty-four hours he would no longer be authorized to wear the uniform.

The bus slowed, its passengers rocking gently with the off-and-on touch of brakes, as the driver steered the vehicle close to the curb in front of Venson's Drug Store, which served as the Adamsville bus station. The paunchy driver glanced at his watch. It was 11:05, and he was running late.

"Okay, everybody. Let's make it snappy. I've got to get this buggy back on schedule." He frowned, looking again at his watch.

Pusser, the only passenger getting off, grabbed an overnight bag, his sole belonging, and hurried down the aisle. He stepped from the bus into a cool, sunny day. He stood for a moment looking up and down the empty streets, then walked to the city police station to see if his father was working the day or night shift. He found him bent over an old, scarred, wooden desk in the station, filling out an arrest report.

"Well, I'll swear and be damned, Buford, we didn't expect you home for another week," Carl Pusser said laughing, as he pulled himself out of a straight-backed chair to grasp his son's hand. "How in the world are you? Do you feel all right? You look strong as a bull yearling."

"I feel that good, too. I don't know why the Marines had to discharge me just because of a little asthma. My health is as good now as it was the day I joined."

Sadness flickered across Buford's dark brown eyes.

"I always said them military doctors were quacks. If they were worth a damn, they'd get out of service and open their own offices instead of living off us taxpayers," Carl said. "Say, you kind of slipped in on us, didn't you? Your mother got a letter from you yesterday telling about your discharge, but it didn't say a word about you coming home today."

"When I wrote the letter, I didn't know I was coming home today, either. In the Marines, they don't tell you anything until the day they want you to do it," Buford said with a grin. "How's things around town? You putting very many people in jail?"

"Nahh. Mostly drunks. Once in a while I have to settle a family squabble or arrest a speeder. Everything stays pretty peaceful."

"Boy, I sure was surprised when Mom wrote about you being appointed police chief. Made me feel real proud."

Carl Pusser's chest swelled. More than anything else, he wanted his youngest son to respect and admire him. He knew Buford was close to his mother, but this was mostly his own fault, he told himself. He had been forced to spend a lot of time away from home in recent years to make a living and hadn't had a real opportunity to get acquainted with his son, but all of this would change now.

"I'm glad you're proud of me, Buford, but most of all, I'm glad you're home to stay."

"How's Mom?"

"She's fit as a new fiddle. Still working over in Savannah. She usually gets home round five o'clock."

"I think I'll drive over and see her."

"That's a good idea. All she's talked about is you coming home."

Buford left his father at the station and went home, staying only long enough to leave his bag.

The six-year-old Chevrolet he had bought in Oklahoma was standing in the yard. He got into it, started the engine and let it idle. Satisfied that it was running all right, he drove out of the yard.

Savannah was nine miles from Adamsville, and he drove it quickly, pulling up in the parking lot of the Dillon Manufacturing Company where his mother worked.

He found her with no trouble, and Helen was so excited about seeing him that she clocked out for the day and went back to Adamsville with him. She made no mention of how fast he drove, he noticed, smiling.

Buford wore his uniform the rest of the day, dreading bedtime, when he would have to put it away. Since it was his first day home in many weeks, he felt that he had to spend most of his time with the family, so there was little chance to show off the uniform in public.

That night, as his mother watched quietly, he took off the coat and laid it neatly across the bed.

"This uniform and the hundred dollars the Marines gave me are the hardest things I've ever had to work for in my life," he said softly, loosening his tie. "And I only got to wear the uniform one time after going through all that hell in basic training and the hospital."

"I've always told you, Buford, that everything works out for the best for them that believe and trust in the Lord. God has a place for you in this life, and it wasn't in the Marines. You've got to be patient."

*   *   *

Buford Pusser's venture into the world had been cut short too soon. Again he was restless and moody. With his military career shattered by sickness, he needed a new goal. He thought about enrolling in the Freed-Hardeman College at Henderson. The school, which was supported by the Churches of Christ, was located in Chester County less than thirty miles away. He could live at home and drive back and forth, which would reduce expenses. But with the holidays so near, he thought it best to wait until after the first of the year to check enrollment procedures. He had to do something, though, to keep the restlessness away.

He decided to get away from the daily grind around the Pusser house in Adamsville and visit his sister in Memphis. It had been almost four months since he had seen Gailye, an attractive brunette who worked at the Mid-South Title Company.

On the afternoon of November 25, Buford talked

Billy Earl Christopher, a close friend, into driving him to Gailye's Memphis apartment. When the two boys arrived, Gailye hugged and kissed her brother and told him he was getting better looking every day. Buford, embarrassed, grinned and waited for Billy Earl to make some kind of a remark, but he kept silent.

Pusser told his sister about his illness in the Marines, about how he had surprised everyone at home by walking in unannounced, and about how she should have seen him in his uniform. Gailye let Buford do most of the talking, and she was careful not to mention anything about his future plans. She knew that this would be a touchy subject with him now, especially after his disappointment.

It was shortly after midnight when Buford and Billy Earl told Gailye good-bye and headed back toward Adamsville. Rain began sprinkling the windshield of Christopher's car soon after they left the city limits of Memphis. He flipped on the wipers.

"Looks like we're going to get a shower," Christopher said. "Farmers sure could have used a good rain back in July, but they don't need it now, and neither do we."

"Yeah, sure makes it rough driving," Buford agreed.

Suddenly, two strong beams of light cut through the half-moon path of the wiper blades and broke into fragments against the raindrops. Christopher squinted against the onrushing lights, jerked the steering wheel to the right and felt the car leave the pavement.

"Hold on, Buford, that guy's run us off the road," Christopher yelled, struggling to keep the car under control. But in spite of his effort, the vehicle flew over the road's shoulder and plunged into the darkness. The noise and falling and spinning seemed endless. When it stopped, Buford Pusser lay motionless in a patch of knee-high weeds near the wreckage.

Christopher, who had escaped injury, ran to Pusser, who was lying on his side. The edge of the road was soon lined with the cars of curious drivers.

"Buford! Buford! Can you hear me?" There was only a moan in answer. "Call an ambulance. This man's hurt," Christopher said to a bystander. He got a jacket from the wrecked car and held it above Buford's face to keep away the rain.

"Ohhh. My back—my back," Buford mumbled, his face distorted with pain. At least he was alive, Christopher thought.

"Take it easy, Buford, and don't move. You're going to be all right. Just don't move."

The wail of sirens pierced the steadily falling rain, and then, strange hands tugged to lift Buford onto a stretcher.

His back felt as if it were on fire, and sharp pains shot into his neck and head. As the ambulance sped toward Baptist Hospital in Memphis, he felt sure that his back was broken. With his nineteenth birthday less than three weeks away, he was overwhelmed with the fear of death, but it was only the beginning; death was to become his constant companion.

CHAPTER IV

"I've Got to Get a Job"

For Buford Pusser, waiting in Baptist Hospital for his back to heal, his room seemed like a cell submerged in a sea of ether and alcohol. He felt trapped by the view outside his window. Days crawled by. Sullen and moody, he accepted the long string of pills and needles without any real hope that his condition would change. On rare occasions when the pain diminished, he tried to joke with the nurses, but his heart wasn't in it.

His mother and Christopher visited him on weekends, and Gailye dropped by almost every day. But still he felt alone, cut off, and restless. He was tired of the hospital room, tired of being cooped up day after day, week after week, in a drab cubicle. He was tired of the things life had given him so far.

Thanksgiving came and went, and signs of Christmas began to appear in the city. Colored lights were strung across downtown streets, and outside his window, Buford could see decorations in the windows of buildings and could hear the steady jingle of bells over Salvation Army kettles on the streets below. He marked his nineteenth birthday and wondered if he would ever be well again.

His nurses, worried about his depression, tried to brighten his spirits by decorating his room. They kept a table near his bed covered with boxes of candy, baskets of fruit and an assortment of nuts. One of the nurses even put up a small, aluminum tree and draped it with a string of blue lights. The greeting cards he received every day were tacked around the door.

The room was more cheerful, but the new atmosphere did little to change his mood. He continued to go over the past and worry about the future. What could it hold for him now, he wondered. He felt death in the season, watching the year coming to an end, and he withdrew from those about him, saying little and smiling less. Confined to the hospital bed, with his movements hampered by bandages and back supports, he grew physically weak.

Christmas Day brought relatives, friends and gifts, and for the first time since he had been wheeled into the hospital's emergency room on the ambulance stretcher, Buford felt a touch of happiness. But when the visitors left, his lightheartedness went with them.

On New Year's Eve, he remembered the parties back home, the exploding firecrackers, booze and laughing girls and midnight kissing. He didn't think he would ever be able to go to another New Year's party, or any other gathering, for that matter.

A visit from his doctor the next day changed his mind—and gave his whole outlook on life a brief lift. Dr. William Shultz, a slender, pale-complexioned man in his early thirties, told Pusser his back had mended well and he would be able to go home in a couple of days. On January 4, 1957, Buford was discharged from the hospital.

*   *   *

While he was recuperating around his father's house, Buford brooded over the turn of events. Though he was no longer confined, now he felt trapped by inactivity and boredom.

"I must have been born under a bad sign. Everything I do turns out wrong," he complained bitterly.

Helen Pusser, who was cleaning her rimless glasses with the bottom of her apron, stopped and looked up.

"Don't talk like that, Buford. 'The Lord works in mysterious ways . . .' and He knows what's best for all of us."

"Well, I wish He'd hurry and up and decide what's best for me. I'm getting tired of waiting."

Mrs. Pusser slipped on her glasses.

"You've got to be patient, Buford. I've told you this many times. The Lord will act when He sees fit, not before. Besides, the doctor told you to take it easy and get a lot of rest."

"I don't care what the doctor said. I need to find a job. I've been thinking about asking Shackleford for one. Driving ambulances should be pretty easy work."

"Buford, you should forget that idea. Driving those things is awful dangerous."

Buford smiled. He remembered the first time he had driven to town, with his mother telling him every move to make. He knew that when she thought of danger on a road, she automatically thought of speed.

For more than a month, Buford stayed close to home. Then one night toward the end of February he decided to make another trip to the state line. Anything was better than sitting around. When his mother asked about his plans for the night, he told her that he was going to a movie with a friend. He didn't like to lie to her, but it was better than having her worrying about him all evening.

Buford drove his Chevrolet around town, looking for someone who might like to go with him to the strip. Apparently everyone had something else to do, and after driving around for half an hour or more without finding anyone, he headed for the strip alone.

The neon lights of the Plantation Club glittered like splinters of colored glass in the slow-falling rain. The air was crisp, and fog hovered over the nearby swampy bottoms.

The club, owned by W. O. Hathcock, Louise's brother-in-law, was located beside U.S. 45, just inside the Mississippi line.

Automobiles, both e x p e n s i v e and cheap, were

parked around the club and along the shoulders of the highway. Pusser slowed his Chevy, searching for a vacant spot. He found an empty place on the far side of the graveled parking area.

As Buford slid out of his car, he heard a woman's voice.

"Oh Bill, I love you! I love you!"

Pusser glanced over into a car parked next to his and saw a couple in the front seat. He could see that neither the man nor the woman had on a stitch of clothing.

Buford was disgusted. The couple should have had enough decency to rent a motel room, he thought, or if they were broke, they should have found a backwoods road. The Shamrock Motel was only a few feet away and seldom-used roads were everywhere.

Tonight, he thought as he walked across the dark parking lot, the state line's jumping, the "thrill seekers" are happy. He remembered his last trip to the line, the scene still preserved in his mind—he saw again the lifeless body of the sailor lying in a pool of blood on the floor of the White Iris Club; Louise Hathcock's cruel smile after she had killed him with a claw hammer; the unconcerned, even amused look on the face of the deputy sheriff.

For a moment, he wondered why he had even wanted to come again. Then he admitted to himself that he, like the others there that night, had been lured to the strip by a desire for excitement that overshadowed his better impulses.

Hearing the music and raucous laughter from within the club, Buford hesitated in front of the door. He ran his hands through his rain-dampened hair, then went into the crowded club, lingering close to the door while he looked around the room for an empty table.

A skinny redhead in dirty Levis staggered up and tried to drag him onto the dance floor. Music was booming out of the jukebox: "Four walls to hear me . . . Four walls to see . . . Four walls to hear me . . .. Closing in on me. . . ."

Buford pulled himself free.

"Come on, let's dance, handsome."

"I don't want to dance."

"O'kay, don't dance—see who cares," she slurred in a drunken voice and lurched away from him. A slender waitress in a skintight dress came toward him.

"Having a little trouble?" she asked.

"Nah, just some drunken broad trying to find someone to dance with," Buford said, with a grin.

"Want a table?"

"Yeah."

"O. K., follow me."

Pusser watched the easy play of hips against the clinging fabric as the waitress wove through the crowd to an empty table near the back. He liked what he saw. He ordered gin and soda and looked again at the girl. He heard loud noises, mixed with the clatter of dice, from a back room.

Pusser still had about seventy-five dollars of the

mustering-out pay from the Marines, and he toyed with the idea of trying to increase the amount.

"Wonder if I could get in the game back there?" he asked the waitress as he ordered another drink.

She looked at Pusser and saw a country boy trying to get in a last fling before spring plowing began. The boys in the back wouldn't mind taking his money along with that of the other suckers already playing.

"I don't know. Wait a minute and I'll find out for you."

The waitress rapped softly on the door of the room and was let in by a fat, balding man. Buford sat, turning his glass around and around on the table.

In a few minutes, she came back and told him he had been cleared.

"Thanks," he said and passed through the door she was holding open.

The room was brightly lighted, crowded and smoky. A poker game was in full swing at a green felt table next to one wall, and a husky man with thinning hair was dealing blackjack at another table on the opsite side of the shabby room. In the middle, several patrons were gathered around a long, narrow dice table.

"What's your game, boy? Dice or cards?"

"Dice."

Pusser moved closer to the table, which was covered with one and five-dollar bills. There were even a few tens and twenties, he noticed.

"Ten dollars you don't eight," said a tall, well-dressed man.

"I'll take that bet," snapped a gray-haired drunk, as he shook the dice in a plastic cup.

"Come on, eighter from Decatur, be there, baby," he pleaded, rolling the dice. The two red squares scrambled against the end board of the table and spun to a stop with four white dots showing on one of them and three on the other.

"Son of a bitch—craps," the drunk muttered, stepping back to let Pusser take his place.

Buford rolled the dice around in his hand, studying them closely. Then he threw a seven for six dollars. He let the money ride as he tossed another seven. Next, he picked up four for a point and made "Little Joe" for twenty-four dollars.

On his fourth roll, Buford crapped out before making a ten. The dice kept changing hands, and Pusser kept fattening the wad of bills in his hand. The next time his turn came around, he flipped out two natural sevens in a row.

"That boy's hung-up on sevens," someone grumbled.

On his third toss, a house man grabbed the dice, pretending to check them.

Buford felt himself grow tense.

"Okay, I saw you switch dice. Let's just keep playing with the other ones," he said, anger creeping into his voice.

All of a sudden, four good-sized men grabbed him and pulled him away from the table. They hit him hard with their fists, and Buford tasted blood. He fell to the floor, unable to defend himself, and felt a sharp kick in his side.

"We'll teach you goddamned plowboys to come over here and accuse us of cheating," one of them yelled, grinding his shoe in Pusser's face.

Buford could feel them going through his pants pocket looking for money. With his dice table winnings, he thought he had about two hundred dollars. When the men were through looking, three of them picked him up, opened the back door and threw him out onto the gravel driveway. It was still raining.

As he lay sprawled face down in the gravel and rain, half-conscious, Buford could think only of getting even with the bastards someday. They had gotten away with robbing, beating, and killing people long enough, he thought. For too many years, they had done as they pleased without any interference from the law.

Struggling to his knees, Buford touched his head with a hand that felt like lead. He pulled a handkerchief out of his back pocket and pressed it against a long gash on the side of his head. Watching the rain mix with his own blood on the ground where he had lain, Buford felt no fear, only anger.

"The sons of bitches will pay for this," he mumbled to himself. "They'll pay for every drop of blood I lost tonight."

He staggered to his car and rested a moment, then drove to the Humphrey-Phillips Clinic in Selmer. When he finally went home, he had 192 stitches in his head and face. His mother was frantic, and he wished more than ever that he hadn't lied to her.

*   *   *

Early in April, Buford followed up his plans for getting a job with the Shackleford Funeral Home, which had establishments in Selmer, Adamsville, Bolivar and Savannah. If he were hired, he hoped to be able to work in Adamsville and Selmer, rotating between the two towns.

He telephoned Marvin Hailey, manager of the Selmer office, and was told to stop by the office for an interview.

The next evening, Pusser, who seldom wore a coat, dressed up in a light blue suit, white shirt, and wide, red tie. With a cotton rag, he dusted off his Marine-issued black slippers, then drove to Selmer.

Buford quietly entered the funeral parlor in Selmer. Someone had died and he saw members of the family huddled close to a grey, cloth-covered casket in a side room. He tip-toed down the carpeted hallway to the office, where he found Hailey, a tall, slender, dark-haired man, studying some business reports.

"Hello, Buford," the mortician said in a low voice. "Just have a seat there in that chair next to the desk. You doing all right?"

"Yes, sir," Buford whispered. It just didn't seem right to talk loud in a funeral home, he thought.

"Well, I must say. You've been pretty lucky."

"Yes, sir. I reckon so."

Pusser had known Marvin Hailey for a long time, but he had never really looked at him before. Now he noticed the pale grey skin and the busy look of his eyes.

"I thought maybe you'd had enough of ambulances by now," Hailey said, with a grin. Buford was not amused.

"Yes, sir. I've had enough of riding in the back of them."

Hailey laughed.

"You a pretty good driver?"

"Yes, sir. I've been driving since I was thirteen."

"You weren't driving when you boys had that wreck up toward Memphis, were you?"

"No, sir. Billy Earl Christopher was driving."

"I guess your back is doing all right now?"

"Oh, yes, sir. It doesn't bother me any at all now."

The mortician rubbed his chin with his hand.

"Well, the job we have open not only includes driving an ambulance, but also helping with funerals."

"I don't mind that. Be glad to help any way I can."

"Okay. We pay a hundred and sixty dollars a month, plus commissions for each funeral."

"When do I start?"

"Tomorrow morning."

Buford started driving one of the Cadillac ambulances for Shackleford the next morning, learning to thread his way through traffic jams as he raced to the scene of an accident or to answer a sick call. He already knew how important it was to exercise care in lifting the injured onto stretchers. He also worked closely with Hailey in the conducting of funerals. His polite, gentlemanly manner blended well with the atmosphere. Some nights while he was waiting around the funeral home, he watched Hailey, studied his professional techniques, and talked with him about his work. Sometimes he thought he might like to be a mortician himself.

He enjoyed the work—driving ambulances, being a part-time pallbearer, comforting grief-stricken family members after burials, and performing all of the other tasks that went with the job. But he didn't like the pay. The most he had made in one month was three hundred dollars, and he had worked especially hard that month in order to earn that much. He had expected the funeral commissions to be much higher than they had been.

Other McNairy County boys had gone to Chicago after high school and had come back talking excitedly about their high-paying jobs. One Saturday afternoon, Buford met Jerry Wright, a friend who was home from Chicago for the weekend. Wright was driving a late model car and wearing expensive clothes. Or, at least, they looked expensive, Buford thought.

"Looks like you're doing all right for yourself, Jerry."

"You ain't wrong, Buford. I never made so much money in all my life. You can make more dough in

Chicago in a week than you can make here in a month."

"You still working at Union Bag?"

"Yep. I make about six hundred a month."

"Six hundred a month! That's unbelievable."

"You can make it, too. In fact, Union Bag is hiring right now."

"They are?"

"Yep."

"Well, I just might be up to see you shortly. I could sure use that kind of money."

"Come on up. I'll put in a good word for you at Union Bag."

"Okay. Be making room for another McNairy County boy up there."

Wright didn't expect his friend to quit his funeral home job and come to Chicago because he didn't think Buford would be willing to break his close ties to home. He was wrong, however. Late in August, Buford turned in the keys to his Shackleford ambulance, drew his final paycheck and left for Chicago.

Wright introduced him to Union Bag Company officials, and he was quickly hired to operate a die-cutting machine. He was pleased with his new salary, which was almost three times the amount he had made at Shackleford's. For the first time, he felt encouraged. Maybe he had finally made the right decision.

Buford was enthralled with the rhythm of the city and the masses of people on the streets. All night he heard police cars or ambulances and he wondered where they were going, if someone had been killed. There was something about dying that intrigued him, and he realized that McNairy County was no different from Chicago as far as death was concerned.

In an effort to better understand his fascination with death, Buford enrolled in Worsham's College, a mortician's school. He was by no means sure that he wanted to be an undertaker, but he had to find out. He continued to work the day shift at the paper mill while he was attending school at night. Though his busy schedule consumed most of his time, occasionally he would drop by his favorite bar for a cold beer.

Sometimes during his tavern visits a brawl would erupt, and he would think again of his experiences at the Plantation Club the night he had been beaten and left to die and at the White Iris when he had seen Louise Hathcock beat the sailor's head in with a claw hammer. He could still see the nonchalant look on that deputy sheriff's face. On those occasions when the scene flitted through his mind, he was again consumed with anger.

After two months, Buford began to get the feel of the city. He discovered that people there went to work, minded their own business, and lived individual lives. Many Chicago residents were not overly friendly, he thought, and they never invited you to their homes for dinner like people in McNairy County did. Some people, he was sure, could live next door to a family for years and never even know their neighbors' names. It was a strange way to live.

Buford followed the trend. He went to work, ate most of his meals in cheap restaurants, and continued to attend the morticians' school. His major social activities were occasional parties with Wright and Marvin King, Jr., another McNairy County boy who was employed at Union Bag. The conversations at these parties were always the same. "Wonder what's going on back home?" someone would say, and they would be off on another evening of reminiscing. Because of Buford's college schedule, however, he seldom got the opportunity to be with Wright and King, and he could find nothing in common with any of the other workers or with students at Worsham's.

Eventually, the strain of keeping up with his studies at college and working a full work shift at the mill became too much. The schooling was also depleting his finances, and after nine months of study, he left Worsham's College.

*   *   *

In 1958, Buford found a new way to earn extra money and at the same time keep in top physical shape. He began wrestling professionally on weekends. A tall, muscular specimen, Buford was a natural crowd-pleaser. He liked the noise, the rough talk, and hard falls. He also did not mind the pretty girls who were usually somewhere in the crowd.

Buford could not look upon wrestling as an actual sport; he thought of it more as an exhibition, a show, which provided good entertainment. He rehearsed in the dressing room to decide which falls who would win and discussed the details of each match at length with his so-called opponent, but despite the lack of suspense, he enjoyed wrestling.

As he came out of his dressing room one night in Chicago, he ran squarely into a petite blonde. He immediately recognized her as being one who had sat a few rows back from the ring that night, cheering enthusiastically.

"Excuse me, Miss. I wasn't paying a bit of attention to where I going."

"That's O. K. I wasn't, either, so I guess we're both partially to blame." She smiled, and Buford had never seen such a smile.

"Hey, I saw you at the match tonight," he said. "Did you like it?"

"I sure did. I love wrestling."

"I'm Buford Pusser."

"I know."

"What's your name?"

"Pauline Mullins."

"I was just on my way to grab a bite to eat. How about joining me?" The blonde hesitated.

"I'm not hungry, but I'll have a cup of coffee while you eat," she said, looking at her watch. "Can't stay

Buford and Pauline on their wedding day.

long, though—got to pick up the kids pretty soon."

Buford was disappointed, but then he glanced at the blonde's left hand. No rings.

"Oh, don't worry," she laughed softly. "I'm not married."

He made no effort to hide his relief.

During his brief visit with Pauline Mullins at a nearby steak house, Buford learned a great deal about her. She was from Haysi, Virginia, divorced, had a small son and daughter, was three years older than he, and, most important of all, she did not have a steady boy friend.

From that time on Buford Pusser was no longer lost and lonely in the big city. He spent as much time as he possibly could with Pauline and her two children, Diane, nine, and Mike, seven. Buford soon became attached to the youngsters and often insisted that he and Pauline take the children with them when they went to a movie or out to eat. The soft-voiced, bright-eyed Pauline and her affectionate children soon became a real part of Buford's life, bringing him a kind of happiness he had never known before. It did not take him long to realize that he was in love and that he wanted to spend the rest of his life with Pauline, Diane and Mike.

On December 5, 1959, Buford and Pauline were married in a quiet ceremony before a justice of the peace. The wedding took place just seven days before Buford's twenty-second birthday.

Buford adjusted quickly to married life. He was no

longer alone; he had a family to come home to, and the small apartment seemed a long way from the "state line."

On the night of January 4, 1960, however, less than a month after their marriage, there was a loud knock on the Pusser's apartment door.

"I'll get it, honey," Pauline said.

She opened the door and peered outside at two well-dressed men.

"Chicago Police, lady. Is this where Buford Pusser lives?"

Buford pushed his way in front of Pauline.

"I'm Buford Pusser. What's the trouble?"

"Well, Mr. Pusser, we've got a warrant here from Corinth, Mississippi, for your arrest," one of the detectives said.

"On what charges?" Pusser asked, looking from one face to the other.

A big man, wearing a trench coat and a narrow-brimmed hat, leaned closer to the porch light and read the summons.

"It says here that they got you charged with armed robbery and assault with intent to commit murder against W. O. Hathcock at the Plantation Club on December 13, 1959."

"That's crazy as hell. I haven't been out of Illinois in months. How could I have been in Mississippi on December 13 or any other time near that?"

"You'll have to thrash that out with them down there, Mr. Pusser. Our job is to arrest you for Alcorn,

Mississippi, authorities and hold you in jail until they get here, so let's go."

Pusser was handcuffed and taken to the Chicago city jail. There, he was photographed, fingerprinted, and labeled a lawbreaker.

Later, a fat policeman accompanied him on a slow-moving elevator to the cell wing. They stepped off the elevator and entered a small room which was enclosed with wire-mesh screen. The only furnishings in the cubicle were a metal desk, a steel chair and a filing cabinet.

"Empty your pockets on the desk there," the police-man said. "The only thing you can keep is your cigarettes and lighter."

"I don't smoke."

"That's good. Wish I didn't. I'd probably feel a lot better and I know I'd have a lot more money. Cigarettes are expensive."

Pusser didn't answer, but he was thinking at the time, he couldn't care less if the overweight cop keeled over from cigarette smoking and went broke trying to feed his nicotine habit.

The tall, bitter Tennessean hated everyone at the moment. The nerve of those bastards at the Plantation Club, he thought. Beating the hell out of him and throwing him out the door, leaving him in a cold rain to die, then having him arrested for robbery and attempted murder. When it was all over, he said to himself, they'd wish they'd never heard of Buford Pusser.

"The sergeant says you don't have to change into jail duds." The officer grinned as he stuffed Pusser's billfold and some loose change into a manila envelope. "He mentioned something about the Mississippi boys coming for you tomorrow or the next day."

The police led Buford down a hallway to a cell which had four bunks and three prisoners. There were upper and lower bunks on each side of the door. The inmates were sitting on the two lower bunks, talking.

The cell door sprang open with the twist of the key, then was slammed shut and Buford was locked inside.

"Welcome to the club, buddy." The man who spoke was a middle-aged Negro. "What's the rap they pinned on you?"

Pusser gripped the cold bars, and tension corded the backs of his hands.

"Some bastard down in Mississippi had me picked up on a robbery and assault with intent to murder charge."

"Man, that ain't good. That charge packs a lot of time."

"I'm not worried. I can prove I wasn't even in the state at the time they say I was. It's a frame-up."

"I hope you're right. It's bad enough to go to prison for somethin' you did but worse to go for somethin' you didn't do."

Pusser didn't answer, but kept looking coldly through the bars into the empty hallway. This had to be a frame-up, he thought. There was no way they could make the charge stick. Yet, he was worried.

Alcorn County Sheriff Hillie Coleman and his brother, Chief Deputy L.W. Coleman, arrived in Chicago January 7, 1960, to take Pusser back to Mississippi. When Buford stepped off the elevator that morning to be taken into custody, however, he was surprised to find that he would not be the only one making the trip. His two friends, Jerry Wright and Marvin King, Jr., were waiting. They, too, had been arrested on the same charges that had been lodged against him.

Before leaving the jail, the three men were handcuffed and shackled by the sheriff and his brother.

"You don't have to chain us up like wild animals," Buford protested. "We don't have any reason to run. We're innocent."

"Shut your goddamned mouth," the sheriff snapped. "And let's get one thing straight before we leave. As far as I'm concerned you all ain't nothing but three two-bit thugs—and that's exactly the way you're going to be treated."

"We're supposed to be innocent until proven guilty, not the other way around," Pusser said.

"Big deal. So now, you're trying to tell me what the law is, huh? Well, let me tell all three of you something. You all are going back to Corinth and stand trial and, as I see it, there ain't a chance in hell of you smart asses missing the penitentiary at Parchman. I figure you'll all get a long stretch behind bars."

Pusser rubbed his wrists, which were being irritated by the handcuffs.

"I thought a jury decided who was innocent and who was guilty," he said. "We can prove we weren't even near the Plantation Club on December 13. No jury is going to send us to prison on hearsay evidence."

"I told you once, Pusser, to shut your goddamned mouth. If I have to tell you again, I'm going to close it with a pistol butt." Buford believed him.

As the sheriff's cruiser sped south with its three prisoners, Buford Pusser saw his dream of a happily married life fading with the Chicago skyline.

CHAPTER V

"We Plead 'Not Guilty'"

Through the car's windshield, Pusser, Wright, and King eyed with cynicism and fear the cracked and deteriorating facade of the Alcorn County Jail. They realized they might be behind the barred windows of the old, gray-brick building for a long time if Hillie Coleman had a say in the matter. Coleman had a plan, they felt; his words in front of the Chicago jail— "There ain't a chance in hell of you smart asses missing the penitentiary at Parchman."—still rang clearly in their ears. Coleman seemed too cocky and confident not to have some kind of trap ready for them.

The sheriff braked the car near the front door of the county jail and climbed out.

"Come on over to this side, L.W. We'll take the bastards out this back door," he said.

The chief deputy hurried around the front of the car.

"Okay, tough boys. Pile out," the sheriff ordered, jerking the car door open.

The three manacled men wiggled like worms across the back seat and slid out the same door. Inside the jail, they were unshackled and taken to a cell on the second floor. They were denied the use of the telephone and the right to post bond.

"Look, Coleman, we've got some rights. You're supposed to let us make a phone call," Pusser complained.

"I told you about your mouth, Pusser. It's going to get you into a heap of trouble," Coleman said. "You don't tell me a goddamned thing. Hear? As far as I am concerned, you and your two sidekicks ain't got no rights. So keep your mouth shut and everything will be just fine."

"We still want to use the phone."

"Big deal. People in hell want ice water too. But they don't get it. Like I said, shut your mouth and quit asking for favors, 'cause you ain't getting none."

*   *   *

For more than a week, Coleman tormented the three men with his sarcastic remarks. "It's going to be hot as hell down there in those cotton fields at Parchman Prison," he said over and over.

"Who gives a damn about Parchman?" Buford snapped. "We're not going there anyway."

"Oh yeah? You're all going. There ain't no doubt about that. And after you all have been there awhile, you'll think ole Hillie Coleman is an angel compared to them prison guards they've got down there. They don't take no shit at all."

"We're not worried," Pusser lied. "We won't even see Parchman."

"Just remember. None of the prisoners down there ever planned on seeing the joint either, but they did." Coleman laughed, walking down the stairs to his office.

"That bastard," Pusser mumbled. "He sure likes to mess with a man's mind."

"Yeah, he gets his kicks that way," King added. "He's got a warped brain."

On January 19, 1960, Pusser, King and Wright were taken out of their cell by the sheriff and driven three blocks to the courthouse for a hearing before District Judge Raymond T. Jarvis.

The judge, a husky man with gray-streaked dark hair, read the charges.

"You three men are charged with robbing W. O. Hathcock, Jr., of $1,176 at the Plantation Club on December 13, 1959. Also, on the same date, you are charged with attempting to murder him. How do you plead?"

All three answered "not guilty."

"Do any of you have any questions?"

"Yes, sir. Who issued the warrants for our arrest?" Pusser asked.

"The warrants were issued by Peace Justice Buck Sorrell on a complaint signed by Mr. Hathcock," the judge said dryly.

"Are we going to be allowed to post bond?"

N.S. "Soggy" Sweat, district attorney, slender, small, in his mid-thirties, arose from behind a nearby table. Sweat, for a reason not known to him, had been nick-named "Soggy" by his schoolmates. He was ambitious and had more pride than a bantam rooster at the county fair.

"Your honor, due to the seriousness of these crimes, I request that these men be held in jail without bond until their trial."

Jarvis picked up a small wooden gavel in his left hand, leaned back in his chair, and gently tapped his opened hand with the gavel.

"I can see no reason to deprive these men of their freedom while they wait trial. I don't believe the evidence in the case is strong enough to justify your request, Mr. Sweat."

"But your honor. We have sworn statements from Mr. Hathcock that Pusser, Wright and King all tried to kill him. We also have statements from other witnesses, including law officers, to substantiate Mr. Hathcock's charges."

"I still do not feel that the evidence is such to deny the three men the right to post bond. I am setting bail at $4,500 on the armed robbery charge and $3,000 on the assault with intent to murder charge."

Sweat slid into his chair.

Judge Jarvis, who had displayed gestures of sympathy toward the accused men during the hearing, was well aware of the state-line activities and the criminal element flourishing there. He detested it. Memories of his dead son might also have strongly influenced his thinking, since young Jarvis had been brutally murdered and buried in a woodshed. Although it had never been officially proven, the judge felt that stateline thugs had been responsible for his son's death. If he were alive, young Jarvis would have been in the same age category as the three defendants.

Buford Pusser posted bond, but King and Wright failed to raise bond money and were returned to jail.

George A. and Clyde King, no relation to the accused King, signed both of Pusser's bonds. The Kings, who owned a farm implement company in Corinth, guaranteed the bonds after being paid $750 by Pusser.

The Alcorn County Grand Jury true-billed Pusser, King, and Wright on January 25, 1960. The armed robbery indictment became Cause Number 8954 and the assault with intent to commit murder bill was tagged Cause Number 8955.

After the indictments, Buford became restless and worried. It had never occurred to him that the Grand Jury would believe the Hathcock tale.

Carl Pusser, whose job as Adamsville police chief had educated him on some of the ins-and-outs of law enforcement, tried to keep Buford's spirits up.

"No use to walk the floor and worry about those sons of bitches over at the state line, Buford. There ain't a jury in the world with a lick of sense that's going to swallow Hathcock's story," Carl assured him. "That whole Hathcock bunch is so low they could crawl under a snake's belly."

"I don't know," Buford said. "Sorrell believed Hathcock enough to issue warrants for our arrest, and the Grand Jury indicted us."

"Hell, that don't mean a damned thing. Sorrell's so crooked he's got to screw his britches on every morning and the Grand Jury is made up of no telling who. The Grand Jury only knows what the district attorney and the law officials say about a case. It's an altogether different story when a real trial jury meets. Remember, your attorney helps pick them, and he ain't about to let some crooked bastard get on the jury."

"Well, I hope you're right."

Buford still had doubts about the trial's outcome, but he didn't let his father know it.

*   *   *

The Alcorn County Courthouse stood amidst a clump of trees in downtown Corinth. An early morning sun cut through the trees and danced off the tan bricks of the building. The sun had bleached the dull gray trim around the windows and roof until it was silvery white. Six gray pillars graced the front entrance of the four-story structure. There was no wind and the flag hung lifeless on a pole near the front walk. Old men, wrapped in tobacco-stained coats, sat on benches along the walk, talked occasionally and whittled cedar sticks. It was January 29, 1960.

"Understand they're pickin' a jury today for them boys' trial who're supposed to have beat and robbed W.O. Hathcock," one man remarked, wiping tobacco juice from an already brown-splotched gray beard.

"Yep. And I shore don't think that case art to have ever gone to trial," replied another. "They art to turn them fellers loose. That state-line bunch ain't nothin' but out-and-out scum of the earth."

"Yore right. If we had any decent law around here, they'd run through them pack of no-goods like General Grant did Richmond."

"I just bet that Hathcock and his gang tried to rob them fellers, and instead, got a dose of their own medicine."

"Shore. That's exactly what happened. If they got any honest folks at all on that jury, they'll turn all three of them fellers scott free."

After a day-long court session on Friday, a jury was seated, and early the next morning, the trial got underway. The state elected to try Pusser and his two friends on the armed robbery charge.

The three defendants sat huddled with Cary Stovall, their attorney, at a long table in the barnlike courtroom on the third floor. Opposite them were Sweat, H. M. Ray, county attorney, and Hathcock.

The jury box was situated on a raised platform on the right side of the judge's bench. The three hundred seats, arranged in a half-circle, were filled. A host of standing spectators filled the courtroom and overflowed out the double doors into the hallway. Four white, fly-specked lamp globes dangled from the ends of long chains suspended from the high ceiling. Two black fans hovered overhead like silent wasps.

In the witness chairs near the front were: Sheriff Hillie Coleman; Lyle Taylor, sheriff at the time of the alleged crime; Constable Cleveland Marlar; Peace Justice Buck Sorrell; Dr. Frank Davis; Mrs. Lorece Hathcock, wife of W.O.; ex-deputy sheriff Perry Rencher; Billy Joe Robinson and Nita Goggins. Both Robinson and Mrs. Goggins were employees of the Plantation Club.

Waiting to testify for the defense were: Mrs. Pauline Pusser; John Howard Pusser, Buford's brother; Elmer St. John, personnel manager for Union Bag Company; Merl Plunk, Pusser's landlord in Chicago; and Jerry Wright's mother.

A bailiff, built like a pot-bellied stove, called out: "The Fifth Judicial Court of Alcorn County, Mississippi, is now in session. The Honorable Judge Raymond T. Jarvis, presiding."

Everyone who wasn't already standing arose from his seat as Judge Jarvis, looking stern in his black robe, entered and took his place on the bench.

The judge sounded his gavel. "Everyone who can, be seated. The rest of you try to make yourselves comfortable. I'm sorry we don't have enough seats to go around," he said. "We're going to have to shut the doors and keep the courtroom as quiet as possible at all times."

The bailiff struggled to close the two wooden doors as several persons elbowed their way into the jammed courtroom. Those who didn't make it scuffled outside the doors for window views.

The first witness for the state of Mississippi was W.O. Hathcock, Jr. A heavyset man with an overstuffed belt line, he looked older than his thirty-three years. He had an aura of confidence about him.

Sweat quickly established that Hathcock owned the Plantation Club and that the nightspot was located near the Tennessee-Mississippi state line in Alcorn County.

"Now, Mr. Hathcock. Will you tell the court what happened on the morning of December 13, 1959?" Sweat asked in a strong voice.

"Well—Buford Pusser, Jerry Wright and this other fellow, whom I later learned was Marvin King, Jr., came into the Plantation Club about 3:00 A.M. and took a seat in the dance hall."

"Why did you recognize Pusser and Wright and not recognize King?" Sweat interrupted.

"Because both Pusser and Wright had been in the club several times before. I recognized them both as soon as they walked in that morning. But I didn't know King."

"Pusser and Wright also stood out in your mind because they were known troublemakers. Right, Mr. Hathcock?"

Stovall sprang to his feet.

"I object, your honor. The district attorney is leading the witness."

"Objection sustained."

"Okay. Now, tell us what happened next, Mr. Hathcock."

"Well, the crowd began thinning out about 5:00 A.M. Pusser, Wright and King waited until everyone had left, then Pusser came up to the bar and asked me if I had a pistol to sell.

"I told him I had a .32-caliber automatic that I'd take $25 for."

"Did Mr. Pusser buy the weapon?"

"Yessir."

"Then, what happened?"

"Pusser and Wright walked a few steps from the bar and began talking. Then King, who was behind me, hit me over the head with a heavy instrument, knocking me unconscious.

"Next, they gagged me with my own handkerchief, looted my pockets, and stole a metal money box from behind the bar."

"When you say 'they,' Mr. Hathcock, you mean Pusser, King and Wright?"

"Yessir. That's correct."

"How much money was stolen from you?"

"$1,176. I had $100 in my pocket and the rest was in the money box."

"How long were you unconscious?"

"I don't know. When I woke up, I went to my living

quarters in the rear of the club and got my wife out of bed. She phoned Dr. Davis, and he told her to rush me to the Corinth hospital."

"And how long did you stay in the hospital?"

"Two weeks."

"Okay. Cross-examine."

Stovall, a slender, red-faced man in his early fifties, a veteran of many courtroom battles, got up from his chair at the defense table and paced slowly back and forth in front of the jury and the witness stand. Occasionally, he glanced at the notes scribbled on a yellow legal pad in his hand. Then he spoke softly.

"Mr. Hathcock. You stated a few moments ago that Mr. King, one of the defendants over there, struck you in the head with an unknown object. You did make that statement, did you not?"

"Yes. King did bash me in the head with something," Hathcock answered coldly.

"Did you see Mr. King come up behind you?"

Hathcock hesitated.

"I asked if you saw Mr. King come up behind you."

"No. But he had to be the one who hit me, because I could see Pusser and Wright, and they were the only three persons in the club at the time other than myself."

"I remind you that all my clients have unquestionable proof that they were not even near the Plantation Club on December 13, 1959. What do you say to that?"

"Naturally, they're not going to admit being at my club. All three of them are bald-faced liars!"

Judge Jarvis rapped the bench with his gavel.

"Mr. Hathcock. I will not tolerate those kind of remarks in my court. You will keep your personal feelings to yourself. Do you understand me?"

"Yessir."

Pusser moved about in his seat, feeling the anger sweeping over him. He wanted to walk up to Hathcock and smash his fat face in. Pusser knew that the club owner would never dare call him a liar to his face. Hathcock was hiding in the shadow of the court.

But the sanctuary was a makeshift one which would soon fall apart. When it did, Pusser would even the score—if he weren't behind bars.

"Okay, Mr. Hathcock," Stovall continued. "You also stated that while you were unconscious, Mr. King, Mr. Pusser and Mr. Wright all gagged you with your handkerchief, rifled your pockets of money, and then stole a metal money box. Is that correct?"

"That's right."

"If you were unconscious, Mr. Hathcock, how do you know who bound and gagged you. Or robbed you?"

A murmur rippled through the crowd, and the jury members exchanged glances. Judge Jarvis gaveled the bench and patiently waited for the room to become quiet.

Hathcock, determined not to let Stovall belittle him, quickly answered.

"Because they were the only persons in my club who could have done it."

"Again, I remind you, Mr. Hathcock. We have only your word that the three accused men were in your club on the morning in question."

"My word's enough!"

"We'll let the jury decide that. I'm finished with this witness," Stovall added.

Sweat instructed Hathcock to seat himself with the other witnesses and then asked Mrs. Lorece Hathcock to take the stand. Mrs. Hathcock, a shapely woman in her mid-twenties with shoulder-length black hair, drew long stares from the men in the courtroom while from the women, she received disgusted glances.

"Mrs. Hathcock," Sweat said politely, "you are the wife of W.O. Hathcock, Jr., owner of the Plantation Club. Right?"

"Yes, I am."

"Did you see the three defendants over there in the Plantation Club on the morning of December 13, 1959?"

"Yes, I did."

"What were they doing?"

"They were sitting around a table drinking beer."

"About what time was it when they entered the club?"

"Around 3:00 A.M."

"How did you happen to know Buford Pusser, Jerry Wright and Marvin King, Jr.?"

"I didn't know Mr. King. I knew Pusser and Wright

because they had been to the club several times before."

"And because of Pusser and Wright's previous visits, you immediately recognized them when you saw them in the Plantation Club on the morning of December 13, 1959. Right?"

"Yes, this is correct."

Sweat looked out across the crowded courtroom, then continued.

"Now, Mrs. Hathcock, tell the jury what happened to your husband on the morning in question."

"Well, I helped with chores around the club until about 4:30 A.M., then I went to our living quarters in the back of the club and went to bed."

"You were alone?" Sweat interrupted. "There were no family members or friends spending the night with you and your husband. Is that correct?"

"I was the only person in our private apartment. We had no guests."

"All right, please continue."

"Well, I went to sleep, and later, I don't know exactly how long it was, W.O. came into the bedroom and woke me up. He was badly hurt and was covered with blood from head to foot. I asked him what had happened and he said Pusser and his two friends had just robbed and beat him. I immediately called Dr. Davis and he told me to rush my husband to the Corinth hospital."

"That is all, Mrs. Hathcock. Thank you. Your witness, Mr. Stovall."

Since Mrs. Hathcock's testimony was almost a carbon copy of the statements made by her husband, Stovall spent little time questioning her.

"You didn't see the defendants strike or rob your husband, did you, Mrs. Hathcock? You have only his word for this. True?"

"I have no reason to doubt his word."

"Please answer the question. You didn't see the defendants strike or rob your husband, did you?"

"No, but like I said, I have no reason to doubt what he told me."

"That's all. Thank you, Mrs. Hathcock."

The district attorney called Dr. Frank Davis to the witness chair. The doctor testified that on December 13, 1959, he had treated W. O. Hathcock for deep head lacerations and severe bruises about the body. He said Hathcock was confined to the hospital for two weeks. Davis added that he was not familiar with any of the details surrounding Hathcock's injuries, nor had he asked about them.

Stovall did not cross-examine.

Judge Jarvis ordered a one-hour recess for lunch; however, for fear of losing their places, few spectators left.

When the trial resumed, H. M. Ray took over the questioning from Sweat. Ray appeared to be out of place in a courtroom. The young county attorney looked more like a minister than a prosecutor.

Ray summoned Hillie Coleman to the witness stand.

"Sheriff, what occasion did you have to see the

defendants on the morning of December 13, 1959?"

"Well, at the time, I was a deputy sheriff. I saw Buford Pusser and his two friends when I made a routine check of the Plantation Club. They were all drinking beer at a table next to the jukebox in the dance hall."

"How did you happen to know Mr. Pusser, Mr. Wright and Mr. King?"

"Well, I didn't really know Mr. Wright and Mr. King. But I knew Buford Pusser. I had seen him in the place several times before. I remembered him because Mr. and Mrs. Hathcock had asked me to keep an eye on him whenever I dropped by the club. They said he was a troublemaker with a chip on his shoulder. And a good-sized guy like Pusser is not easy to forget."

"You checked the club, then left?"

"Yessir."

"Were the three defendants still in the Plantation Club when you left?"

"Yessir."

"Cross-examine."

Stovall walked slowly to the witness box. Then he returned to the defense table and picked up his legal pad. Coleman waited impatiently. Again, Stovall approached the witness stand.

"Sheriff, you stated that you recognized Mr. Pusser because he stuck in your mind as a troublemaker—that Mr. and Mrs. Hathcock had pointed him out to you on previous occasions as a man to watch. Is that correct?"

"That is right."

"Have you ever arrested him for any violation at the Plantation Club or any other club or place?"

"No, sir."

"Then how would you know if Buford Pusser is a troublemaker? You admit that you have never had any problems with him."

"Well, after you've been in law enforcement for awhile, it's pretty easy to spot a troublemaker. I tagged Pusser as one the minute I laid eyes on him, and my opinions were supported by Mr. and Mrs. Hathcock."

"Don't you consider it strange, sheriff, for Mr. Hathcock to sell a pistol to a man he claims to be a troublemaker?"

"I—I don't know that Mr. Hathcock sold Pusser a pistol."

"The court records will show that Mr. Hathcock testified earlier in this trial that he sold a .32-caliber pistol to Mr. Pusser for $25. Isn't this unusual for a club owner to provide a weapon to a man he has branded as a troublemaker?"

Coleman hesitated. He searched his mind for an answer.

"Did you understand my question, sheriff?"

"Yes. I guess this would be kind of unusual. But like I said before, Mr. and Mrs. Hathcock both warned me about Pusser. They asked me to watch him."

Suddenly, Stovall wheeled around and raised his

voice: "Isn't it true, sheriff, that you didn't see Buford Pusser, Jerry Wright or Marvin King in the Plantation Club on the morning of December 13, 1959, that W.O. Hathcock and his wife told you they were there?"

"No—no. That's not true at all," Coleman stammered. "I ought to know if I saw them there or not."

"Yes. I guess so," Stovall replied contemptuously.

The attorney wanted to question the sheriff about the night club being open at such a late hour in the morning, but he knew it had been common practice for years to permit the joints to run wide open all night, so he did not waste time on the subject now. He sat down beside Pusser.

"That bastard's lying through his teeth," Buford snapped. "He's trying to frame us."

"Just take it easy, son. That jury didn't ride into town on a jackass."

"I hope you're right, Mr. Stovall."

Buford Pusser realized Sheriff Coleman was attempting to build a case by claiming to be an eyewitness to their presence in the Plantation Club and instilling in the jurors' minds the idea that Buford was a troublemaker capable of committing any crime.

But Pusser hadn't seen all of Coleman's tactics.

The sheriff's cohorts, Constable Cleveland Marlar and ex-deputy Perry Rencher, also testified that they had seen the three accused men in the club on the morning of the alleged crime. And ex-sheriff Lyle Taylor stated that Coleman informed him shortly after Hathcock was taken to the hospital that Pusser and his two friends were involved in the alleged robbery and beating.

Billy Joe Robinson and Nita Goggins also testified that they had seen Pusser, Wright, and King in the Plantation Club prior to Hathcock's beating. Both of the club employees said they recognized Pusser and Wright from the two men's past visits.

Under cross-examination, like the other state witnesses, they stuck to their stories.

At midnight, Judge Jarvis recessed the court.

"Court is recessed until tomorrow morning at 9:00 A.M. I know it's Sunday, but we need to get this trial over. Maybe the preachers will be as lucky as I have been today and have packed houses," the judge said.

Jarvis expected a near-empty courtroom on Sunday. He knew that many of Saturday's spectators were church-going people, and he hoped that they would slide into a church pew the next morning instead of a courtroom chair. The judge liked quiet trials.

But his expectations failed to materialize Sunday morning. Ministers delivered their hell-and-brimstone messages to a few faithful members, and the judge wound up with another overcrowded courtroom.

The first defense witness was Buford Pusser. Stovall had instructed him to be calm and not to appear bitter or to lose his temper. The defense attorney had impressed upon him the importance of projecting an image of a poor, mistreated victim who had been wrongly accused.

"Mr. Pusser. Please tell the jury where you were on the morning of December 13, 1959," Stovall began.

"I was in Anna, Illinois."

"All right. Now tell us how you came to be in Anna, Illinois."

"Well, about 6:00 P.M. on December 12, 1959, I left Chicago with my wife, Pauline, Marvin King, Jerry Wright and my brother, John. All of us went to a friend's house in Anna, arriving there about 2:00 A.M. on the morning of December 13, 1959."

"How far is Anna from Chicago?"

"About three hundred miles."

"Driving under normal conditions, it would take approximately sixteen hours to drive there and back, even if you did not stop. Correct?"

"Yessir."

"Have you ever been in the Plantation Club?"

"Yessir."

"When was the last time you were there?"

"Last October. Jerry Wright and myself went to the club one night while we were on vacation."

"All right. Since your whereabouts are accounted for during a sixteen-hour period from 6:00 P.M. on December 12 until 10:00 A.M. on December 13, 1959, you couldn't possibly have been in the Plantation Club at 3:00 A.M. on the morning in question, could you?"

"No, sir."

"Cross-examine."

Sweat, who had replaced Ray as prosecutor, studied his notes for a moment.

"Where are you employed, Mr. Pusser?"

"The Union Bag Company in Chicago. I operate a die-cutting machine."

"What time did you leave work on Friday, December 12, 1959?"

"Around 5:00 P.M."

"Did you go straight home?"

"Yes, I did."

"Had you already made plans for a trip?"

"Yes."

"And isn't it true that the trip you planned was to Alcorn County, Mississippi, not Anna, Illinois? That you, Mr. King and Mr. Wright hatched the idea for the Mississippi trip while at work?"

"No. We had planned for several days to visit a friend in Anna."

Sweat paced nervously in front of the witness box like a doomed man awaiting a last-minute reprieve.

"Now, Mr. Pusser. It is plain to see why you carefully planned this trip to the Plantation Club. You had to cover your tracks well. Otherwise, you knew you would be linked to the beating and robbing of W.O. Hathcock because you had every reason to commit this vicious crime—you came back to seek revenge for the beating you received there one night at the hands of some dice players. Isn't this correct?"

Stovall leaped to his feet.

"I object, your honor. The DA is bringing in hear-

say evidence. There are no official records to substantiate his charges."

"Objection sustained. Please stick to the facts in
the case, and not hearsay evidence," Judge Jarvis
ordered. "Also, the court reporter will please strike
the last remark from the records."

Sweat knew he was off base, but he hoped the
jurors had been able to grasp what he was trying to
say—that Pusser had returned to the Plantation Club
to collect an old debt which involved both money and
honor.

The DA failed to break Pusser's story about a pre-
planned trip to Anna, Illinois.

Pusser's testimony was also supported by the statements of his wife, Pauline; his brother, John; King,
Wright and Wright's mother. Merl Plunk, who owned
the Chicago apartment that Pusser rented, verified
the time the group left and the time they arrived back
home.

Elmer St. John, personnel manager for Union Bag,
presented Pusser, King and Wright's time cards showing that all three men had been at work on Friday,
December 12, 1959 and had left work at 5:00 P.M.

St. John also produced pay records which reflected
a yearly earning of more than $7,000 each for the
three accused men.

Stovall, during his final argument to the jury,
quickly put the figures to work for the defense.

"Mr. King, Mr. Wright and Mr. Pusser are far from
being paupers. The report by Mr. St. John clearly

shows this. All three men have good jobs and good salaries. With an income like they have, these men don't have to rob and take a chance on being sent to the penitentiary.

"Also, official time cards of the Union Bag Company prove that they were at work until 5:00 P.M. on December 12, and countless witnesses have testified that Buford Pusser, Jerry Wright and Marvin King, Jr., all left for Anna, Illinois, shortly after getting off work on that date.

"I think you twelve honest citizens of the jury have no choice but to find all three men innocent. I also feel that this will be your verdict. Thank you."

Sweat argued that the stories told by the defense witnesses were "too pat."

"It's as plain as the nose on your face." He smiled at the jury. "The defense witnesses collaborated with the defendants to construct this fictitious tale about a trip to Anna, Illinois.

"But the collaborators overlooked one important thing. They forgot about the eyewitnesses who saw them in the Plantation Club on the morning of December 13, 1959."

Sweat's voice had the ring of a defeated general pleading for understanding from his soldiers.

"You must remember that some of the witnesses who testified to seeing Buford Pusser, Marvin King, Jr., and Jerry Wright on the morning in question wear the badge of justice. They are honest men who believe in law and order.

"Pusser, King and Wright were not in Anna, Illinois, on December 13, 1959. They were at the Plantation Club in Alcorn County, Mississippi, for the purpose of robbing W.O. Hathcock. In the process, they almost killed him. He remained in the hospital for two weeks, recovering from the severe beating administered to him by the three defendants."

The district attorney was silent for a moment. Then quietly he added: "I don't see how you, twelve honest, law-abiding citizens, can reach any other verdict in this brutal case except that of guilty. Thank you for being so patient and for listening to the facts—facts which clearly show the three defendants to be guilty as charged."

The case went to the jury at 6:00 P.M. Sunday. Two hours later, after taking time out to eat supper, the jury returned with a verdict of "not guilty."

Spectators in the courtroom applauded the verdict.

Sweat, although disappointed, congratulated the defendants and Stovall. He still felt that they were guilty.

The DA had heard of Pusser's beating at the Plantation Club during a dice game. There had been no official report of the incident filed, but there had been talk around Corinth about the gambling squabble.

Buford Pusser, Sweat thought, had a perfect motive for the crime. Without records, however, the incident could not be brought up in the trial, and Hathcock didn't want to discuss the matter. The DA understood Hathcock's attitude. After all, he wasn't supposed to be running a gambling establishment and moreover, the DA wasn't supposed to allow such an operation.

N.S. "Soggy" Sweat, however, was already preparing to try Pusser, King and Wright on the charge of assault with intent to commit murder.

CHAPTER VI

"I Want to Go Home"

On U.S. 66 near Chicago, Buford and Pauline Pusser watched the threatening weather closely. Since they had crossed the Illinois line, storm clouds had darkened the sky. Occasionally, a flash of lightning exposed naked, flat fields below, where corn, soybean and wheat stalks rotted in the black dirt. It was February and the air was brisk and damp.

"It's going to rain before we ever get home," Pauline predicted.

"Yeah, dammit. It's bad enough driving in Chicago on dry streets, much less wet ones," Buford complained.

The weather had changed the topic of conversation in the Pusser car. Until now, the trial had dominated their thoughts. Buford had laughed and boasted about making the Hathcock clan liars in public and had gloated over the rebuff of Sheriff Hillie Coleman. Moreover, after talking to Cary Stovall, he felt confident that the assault with intent to commit murder charges would be dropped. After all, if Alcorn County officials couldn't prove that he and the other two were at the Plantation Club during the robbery, how could prosecutors link them to the assault on Hathcock? Both charges had sprung from the same incident. Both Buford and Pauline agreed, however, that he and his friends had been lucky to escape imprisonment.

It was raining hard when Buford parked the car in front of the Pussers' four-room apartment at 1425 North Washtenaw Street in Chicago.

"Whew! It's coming down in washtubs," Buford said, pulling his coat collar up around his neck. "Wake the kids while I open the apartment door. Maybe it'll slack off in a minute."

Pauline shook Mike and Diane, who had slept in the back seat during most of the trip.

"Get up, kids. We're home."

Buford unlocked the door and stepped inside. He felt a sigh of relief, and even though he disliked Chicago, it was comforting, this time, to be back at the place he called home. He brought his raincoat from a closet and turned to see Pauline and the children hurrying through the door.

"If you all had waited a minute, I would have brought you a raincoat to hold over your heads. But you just couldn't wait, could you?"

"Honey, a little water isn't going to kill us," Pauline smiled.

"It might," Buford added. "You could all catch your death of cold."

Pauline didn't answer.

*   *   *

With the excitement of the trial behind him, Buford returned to his job at Union Bag, continuing to wrestle on weekends. The wrestling bouts took him to Philadelphia, Pittsburgh, Cincinnati and other large cities, and on each trip, he missed his family more. Eventually, he began to tire of the long trips and the weekends away from Pauline and the children. He continued to wrestle only because the pay was good and the extra money always seemed to come in handy.

In May 1960, Pusser's morale reached a low point. Things were going poorly on the job. He just couldn't seem to do anything right. The boss complained all the time, the happy-go-lucky attitude of his fellow workers irritated him, and every day seemed like a month.

One evening after work, Buford came into the apartment and slammed his lunchbox down on the kitchen table. He looked up and was embarrassed to see Pauline standing in the doorway of the living room.

"My, you seem to be in a bad mood." Pauline smiled. "You'd better be careful or you'll knock a hole clean through that table top."

"Ahh, I wasn't really paying any attention. I'm just tired."

Pauline put her arms around him.

"Sit down and rest your weary bones. I've got some good news for you."

"Good news? What kind of news could be good?" Buford asked, still standing.

"You, Mr. Pusser, are going to be a father."

"A father! Are you sure? How do you know?"

"The doctor told me today. He said the baby would be born sometime in January."

Buford forgot all of his problems. More than anything else, he wanted a child of his own.

"That's great. Just wonderful. This is the best news I've ever heard. We're going to have a baby!" He said it again and again, each time with more elation. He embraced Pauline and kissed her on the cheek.

"You're not to be liftin' anything heavy around here, or doing a lot of housework. Hear?"

"Yes, master."

"If something needs to be moved, you wait until I get home from work and I'll move it. And that's an order—not a request."

"Yes, master."

Buford Pusser now lived in a different world. He became easier to get along with, less moody. Even the hours he spent at work were more tolerable than they had been in the past.

The final weeks of Pauline's pregnancy were much easier on her than on Buford, who was tormented with anticipation.

Near the end of December 1960, Buford inquired every evening when he returned from work if there was a late word from the doctor. Usually, there was nothing new. The baby was still expected sometime during the first of January, and Pauline was doing fine.

"If I'm at work when you have to go to the hospital, you call me right away. I want to be there when the baby is born," Buford reminded his wife for the hundredth time.

"I will, darling, I will. I want you there, too."

"It seems like it's been years instead of months since you first told me you were pregnant."

"Yes, it does seem like time has passed slowly. What do you want the baby to be, honey? A girl or boy?"

"I don't care. Just as long as it's in good health. I don't really have any favorites when it comes to babies."

Pauline smiled. She loved her husband deeply and considered herself fortunate to have married someone who cared for children as much as he did.

The long period of waiting finally came to an end. On January 9, 1961, at 8:18 P.M., Pauline gave birth to a nine-pound, four-ounce girl in Chicago's Ravenswood Hospital. The baby was named Dwana Aitoya Pusser.

Within a few days, Buford was an expert at warming bottles, mixing baby formulas, and changing diapers.

*   *   *

For more than a year, Buford worked at the paper mill, scuffled with sweating bodies on a canvas, and enjoyed his family when time permitted. Then early in 1962, he realized that whatever it was he was seeking was not in Chicago, nor was it on the wrestling mat. What he sought could be found only at home.

Pauline was not surprised when Buford told her he wanted to go home. She had been expecting it at almost any moment.

"Honey, my home is wherever you are, whether it's McNairy County or here in Chicago. The decision is all yours," Pauline assured him.

"Well," he said, "I can't take this damned life here anymore. I'm fed up with it. Crowded streets, crowded stores, and crowded everything. There's no room to breathe. Besides, most people here don't care if you live or die."

"Like I said, Buford, I'm ready to move when you are. Do you have any idea what kind of work is available back home?"

"No, but I'll find a good job. Don't worry about that!"

Pauline wondered, nonetheless, whether Buford would be able to land a job with an income similar to the one they had been used to in Chicago. After all, it would be hard to cover a silver dollar budget with a dime-sized paycheck. She consoled herself with the knowledge that the move to McNairy County would benefit the whole family. Buford wasn't happy in Chicago, and when he wasn't happy, it was impossible for anyone associated with him to enjoy a peaceful moment. Also, Alcorn County officials had dropped the charge of assault with intent to commit murder against Buford, King and Wright. Pauline expected no further trouble from the state-line gang.

Once Buford had made the decision, he became almost jovial, and his only thought was to accomplish the move as quickly as possible. He gave his two weeks' notice at Union Bag and began mapping plans to leave Chicago. The following weekend he canceled wrestling engagements in St. Louis and Kansas City and went to Adamsville. He rented a house trailer, which was located a short distance from the home of his parents, asked his father to keep an eye open for an available job, and then returned to Chicago.

The morning after his notice at work became final, Buford loaded the family and a few belongings into their Chevrolet and headed for McNairy County. It was going to be good to get home.

*   *   *

The Pussers moved into the house trailer and began adjusting to their new way of life. Pauline enrolled Mike and Diane in the Adamsville Elementary School and Buford scouted the area for work. Employment opportunities, however, were slim; the regular jobs were already filled. Fortunately, Buford had saved most of the earnings from his wrestling bouts, and the family had enough to live on for a few months.

After a couple of weeks of job hunting, Buford decided to start wrestling again. Although the skirmishes on canvas wouldn't make him wealthy, he felt they would at least provide enough money to keep the creditors satisfied until he could get a full-time job.

He wrestled in many West Tennessee towns and his name soon became a household word in Southern wrestling circles. McNairy Countians watched with pride when he performed on television. In West Tennessee, wrestling fans came to believe he could whip any man single-handedly and often said, "Buford Pusser's not scared of the devil himself."

One Saturday afternoon, a circus promoter set up a ring in Savannah and offered a fifty-dollar bill to anyone who could pin a hundred and sixty pound black bear to the mat. Buford accepted the challenge and, along with several other men attracted by the prize, signed up to take on the bear.

While the preliminaries were going on, the bear, with his long snout encased in a muzzle, stood patiently in the center of the ring in an outdoor arena bathed in blue tobacco smoke. Then, one after another the challengers climbed into the ring, but were quickly knocked down by the bear's swinging paws. Buford waited his turn and watched the bear's movements.

Two brothers, who could have passed for twins, were next. Dressed in faded overalls and with long, shaggy black hair, they climbed into the ring to battle the bear. Buford thought they were obviously more at home in the cotton fields than in a wrestling arena.

"Look at that. Ain't them two somethin', beats all I ever seed," a red-headed woman near Pusser said, laughing.

"Ugly as homemade sin," Buford said. "And both drunk as skunks."

"You ain't kiddin' about that. Them two will be lucky to even see that bear," the woman answered.

One of the brothers staggered away from the corner of the ring and tried to hug the bear. The animal slapped him on the side of the head with his paw and sent him sprawling across the canvas. The crowd roared with laughter.

"That bear ain't in no lovin' mood," yelled an old man with a snuff-stained gray beard.

"Yeah, that's right," said another spectator. "However, you might try blowing your breath in his face until you get him dead drunk."

The crowd laughed.

The fallen man was helped up by his brother and the two backed off in a huddle, whispering as if the bear might hear their strategy. Then the other brother tried his luck. The furry animal took a step toward him, and he fell over backwards trying to get out of the reach of a swinging paw. He scrambled to his feet and joined his brother in another whisper session in a far corner of the ring.

"Be careful boys, or that bear might hear you," jeered a spectator. "He's got keen ears and he's smart as a whip."

After being knocked down one more time each, the

brothers decided to take another swig out of the moon-shine jug and leave the bear and the fifty dollars to the next challenger.

Buford Pusser was next in line. His weight topped the bear's by about eighty pounds. He crawled through the ropes, stood and flexed his muscles slightly, while the crowd cheered. His chest swelled with pride. He knew that he had to make a good impression. His "fearless man" reputation was at stake.

The bear, on all four feet, stalked around the far end of the ring, glaring at Buford. Suddenly, it sat up and attempted to rip off the muzzle with its two front paws. When the efforts failed, the bear shook its head frantically.

Pusser moved a little closer. The animal reared up as if to dare Pusser to make a play. Silence fell over the crowd. Without warning, Pusser rushed in and threw a football block into the bear's midsection.

"Whuff!"

The bear grunted loudly as the breath gushed out of him and he tumbled to the canvas. Pusser jumped on top and quickly pinned his muzzled opponent to the mat.

The crowd cheered wildly as Buford slipped through the ropes and courteously brushed aside a throng of well-wishers. He made his way to the pro-moter. The bear's owner, however, hadn't expected anyone to collect the reward, and he fumbled with his billfold for several minutes in an attempt to stall pay-ing Pusser.

"Look, mister. I won that money fair and square. Now I want my loot. You'd better come up with fifty bucks real fast or you and me are going to have a heap of trouble," Pusser threatened.

The promoter fingered a crisp fifty-dollar bill from his wallet and handed it to Pusser. After all, who wanted to tangle with a man who had just floored a bear?

*   *   *

On Monday night after the Savannah circus, Carl Pusser pulled his police car up into Buford's driveway and called him out of the trailer.

"Get in the car a minute, Buford, I want to talk to you. I think it's better that we discuss this matter alone."

"What's the trouble? That damned bear promoter sign a warrant against me for threatening him?" Buford asked.

"Hell, no. You know that bastard, as crooked as he is, ain't going to file charges against anybody."

Both laughed.

"I guess you're right," Buford said. "That's the easiest fifty bucks I ever made, though."

Carl's voice suddenly took on a serious tone.

"Son, my leg's been bothering me a lot lately. It's never been the same since that wreck.

"I've been thinking about quitting this police chief

job. I have to spend too much time on my feet. I think you'd be the ideal man for the job."

In a way, Buford wasn't surprised. His father had threatened for several weeks to turn in his badge. Besides, Carl had walked with a limp and complained of leg pains since October 1957 when a car had run his pickup truck off the road. The truck had turned over, pinning Carl inside.

"I'd sure like to have the job if you quit, but do you think the city board will hire me?"

"Hell, yes. Don't worry about that. I've already talked to the mayor about it, and he's all for you having the job."

"That's good news. Tell him I'm ready anytime you quit."

"I'll tell the mayor tomorrow that you'll take the job. Good night."

Buford entered the house trailer and found Pauline rolling her hair in curlers.

"What was that all about?" she asked, dipping her fingers in a glass of water, then wetting a long strand of blonde hair.

"Dad's legs are hurting him a lot and he's going to quit the police chief's job. He's already talked to Mayor Blanton and they want me to take the job."

Pauline laid down a curler on the coffee table top and stood up.

"That's great, honey. I think you'll make Adamsville a wonderful police chief. It's a good job, too. Shouldn't be much danger involved, either. About all you have to do is arrest a few drunks and stop a few speeders."

"Right. And it pays three-hundred a month. Besides, I can still pick up a few extra dollars wrestling. Of course, the city board will have to approve me."

"I don't think you'll have any trouble getting approved by the council. With Mayor Blanton on your side, you've got it made. He carries a lot of weight with the councilmen." Pauline smiled, standing on tip-toe to kiss her husband.

"I hope you're right. I'd sure like to have that job."

"Don't worry, darling. You'll get it."

Two days later, Mayor Leonard Blanton called the three-man Adamsville City Council together for a special meeting. Blanton, owner of a local construction company, was a man who possessed the rare quality of being able to get along with almost every person he met. The other two board members, J.D. Abernathy and George Tidwell, were not as gifted, but they were honest men who always put the welfare of the city first when weighing city business. Abernathy worked for the state tax department; and Tidwell, an elderly gentleman, owned a grocery store and cotton gin.

Blanton got right down to business and recommended that the board hire Buford Pusser as the town's chief of police.

"I think Buford'll make us a fine police chief," Blanton said. "He is polite and big enough to gain the respect of everyone, including our young people. Also, he's an honest man. I highly recommend that we hire him."

The mayor's remarks drew no protests from either Abernathy or Tidwell, and the vote to hire Buford was unanimous.

The first thing Buford did after taking office was make friends with the teen-agers of the area. Since he was only twenty-four himself, he accomplished his goal with little difficulty.

When the young speeders raced through town, Buford stopped them, and in most cases, handed out advice instead of tickets. His advice was not to get caught again with their "foot in the carburetor," or they would be in serious trouble. Most of them heeded his advice, but there were those who seemed to be born with a natural urge for fast driving. For these, Pusser worked out a special plan.

Late at night, after the streets had cleared and the "old-fashioned" folks had climbed under the covers, Buford took the racing enthusiasts out to a deserted country road. He blocked it off, then turned the drag-racers loose. He always supervised the events and set the rules.

A major rule of the "private racing club" was never to break the speed limit on any public street or highway. Those who did and were caught lost their "membership" in the special late-night club.

The teen-agers grew to admire and respect Buford Pusser. They considered him one of their own.

*   *   *

In September 1962, Buford Pusser decided to seek his first elected office, constable in the Third Civil District. Being a constable was only a part-time job, and if he won, it wouldn't interfere with his present work. He would remain Adamsville's chief of police.

Buford campaigned hard—shaking hands, soliciting votes, and handing out small name cards. He made no special promises except to give the citizens of the district fair and impartial law enforcement.

Carl Pusser, a sly, behind-the-scenes politician, also worked hard gathering votes for his son. He knew a lot of people in McNairy County, and he also knew where the political power lay and how to get it.

Buford's opponent was Tommy Morris, who had held the constable seat for several years and was determined not to let a "young kid" beat him. He harped on Pusser's youth and inexperience, but the voters turned him down when they went to the polls in August. Buford Pusser beat the incumbent constable by more than 115 votes.

Buford kept busy patrolling the streets of Adamsville and keeping an eye on activities in his constable district. He worked long hours, sometimes getting less than three hours sleep in a twenty-four hour period.

In August 1963, however, he was forced to slow his pace when Pauline became ill with hepatitis. The liver ailment kept her in bed off and on for more than a year.

Buford helped twelve-year-old Diane with household chores and with cooking the meals. He enjoyed experimenting with various recipes and often turned out a tasty dish. In fact, Pauline sometimes threatened to turn the job over to him permanently. The chores around the house kept him tied down much of the time, but he always managed to fulfill his police duties.

Late one evening in November, he received a tip about an illegal whiskey still operating in his district south of Adamsville and immediately checked out the information.

The last rays of daylight flickered through the bare tree limbs as he slipped down a narrow, leaf-covered path in the woods. Ahead, he saw smoke drifting through the trees. He stepped on a dead limb and quickly hid behind a huge white oak as the snapping sound echoed through the quiet woods like a rumble of thunder.

Buford waited a minute or two, then eased closer. A short distance away he saw three men standing around a large homemade distillery. Sacks of sugar, hundreds of gallon jugs, stacks of hickory wood, and several fifty-five gallon barrels cluttered the area. A blackened steam boiler was going full blast under the watchful eyes of the three men.

Buford knew that he couldn't pull a raid by himself. Besides, this was his first experience in dealing with moonshiners, although ever since he could remember, homemade distilleries had lined the bottoms of Webb Fork and Sugar Creek in the county. With corn more plentiful than money, smoke from the stills had clouded the skies each evening. Every now and then federal and state revenue agents swooped down on the moonshiners, and on a good day, one or two were jailed. The rest, more often than not, escaped down well-known paths in the woods, and for a few days after a raid, the skies would clear of smoke. Then the moonshining activity would resume with a new fury.

Buford crept out of the woods the same way he had come in. When he got back to Adamsville, he went into his office and telephoned Federal Revenue Agents Stanley Fry and Charles Dickey at Jackson. The agents told him to keep the still under surveillance until they could get to McNairy County, which would probably be in about three days.

Two days after Pusser's telephone call, Fry and Dickey arrived in Adamsville. Methodically, the agents went over plans for the raid with Buford.

"A raid on a still isn't really successful unless you can catch the whiskey-makers there," Dickey said. "Just blowing up an abandoned still doesn't accomplish much.

"The moonshiners can always build another still and start right back to making corn liquor in a few days. But if you catch 'em, they ain't likely to run off another batch of booze for awhile, even if they make bond, because they know the heat is on and they're being watched."

Dickey glanced at his wrist watch and then at the dying sun.

"It's getting late," he said. "Within the next hour or so we should have a good chance of catching them at the still. They'll be getting ready to cook, or may already be at it."

"It was about this time of evening when I saw them at the still," Pusser said, "and they were cooking a batch then."

"Let's go," Dickey ordered.

The three men sneaked through the woods with cat-like movements. Dickey's speculation paid off. The whiskey-makers were busy at their work. Pusser and the agents unholstered their pistols and quietly approached the still site.

"Okay, boys, put up your hands and don't move," Dickey said politely.

All three moonshiners stopped what they were doing and raised their hands.

"This still belong to you fellows?" Fry asked.

"No, sir. We don't know a thing about this here whiskey still," one of the men said. "We were just traipsing through the woods looking for walnuts, when we run smack dab into this thing."

"Bullshit," Pusser snapped. "All three of you guys were at this still the other evening. I saw you here."

The man didn't answer.

Fry and Pusser handcuffed the three men, then led them through the woods while Dickey rigged dynamite sticks under the boiler and mash barrels.

The still had been producing more than three-hundred and fifty gallons of "white lightning" a week.

"Fire in the hole!" Dickey yelled, as he raced toward the men, who stood several hundred yards away. Then there were a series of blasts that shook the ground. The boiler soared above the treetops, twirling crazily in the air, then fell like a bomb-shattered corn silo. The mash covered the tree limbs which began to drip alcohol. Buford Pusser had witnessed his first still raid.

Under normal circumstances, Pusser would have notified Sheriff James Dickey about the illegal whiskey still, and the sheriff would have been responsible for contacting federal or state revenue agents. Pusser, however, didn't trust Dickey. He considered the sheriff to be one of the major links in the chain of state-line activities.

Pusser was sure that Dickey was taking payoffs from the Hathcocks and other racketeers on the strip. Murders, robberies, bootlegging and whore-hopping still flourished there and it was Pusser's personal opinion that Dickey hadn't tried to slow the tempo in any form or fashion. Still thirsty for revenge because of his own unfortunate tangles with the Hathcocks, he began making plans to rid the state line of the hoodlum element. He wanted to do it legally, with the endorsement of law and order.

Buford decided that the best way to accomplish this end was to acquire the top law enforcement seat, so he decided to run for sheriff of McNairy County on the Republican ticket. He discussed the plan with his father, and Carl quickly put his stamp of approval on the idea.

"I think you can beat James Dickey," he said. "He's getting unpopular as hell. Folks all over the county are fed up with him playin' footsie with those crooked bastards at the line."

"Well, I don't know. I may not win," Buford said. "But I'm going to give it a try. That's the only legal way I can run those sons of bitches out of this county."

"You're right, son, and you'll be surprised at the amount of support you'll get from other honest citizens around here."

The elder Pusser became Buford's campaign manager, and he began to solicit funds and votes. Carl, who was an old hand at politics, persuaded Mayor Blanton to raise five hundred dollars for the "Buford Pusser for Sheriff" campaign, and he collected lesser amounts from many other McNairy Countians.

Buford was strangely apprehensive about his new venture. He had no fear of the state-line criminals who had tried to murder him, but he had waited a long time for this opportunity to put them out of business. He was only afraid that the citizens of McNairy County might not elect him sheriff.

CHAPTER VII

"I'm Going to Clean Up the State Line"

Everywhere Buford went during his campaign, he talked simply and to the point about what he would do as sheriff of McNairy County. "If you elect me," he would say in a soft voice, "I will clean up the corruption and violence that has made the state line notorious. I'll make McNairy County a decent place to live and raise a family." Campaigning day and night in all corners of the county, he sought to reach as many of its 18,085 residents as possible. He went to large and small towns, including those that were traditionally Democratic. Republican Pusser was determined to change the voting trend.

Many of the people who heard him speak remembered him as the professional wrestler who had pinned a black bear, and they enthusiastically pledged him their votes. Buford, however, did not take these pledges too seriously. Talk was one thing, but going to the polls was something else. He remembered the

fate of Grand Ole Opry star Roy Acuff, also a Republican, who had lost his bid for the governor's chair a few years before. Acuff had a half-million Tennessee fans at the time, but when it came right down to it, only a few voted for him. Buford was afraid the same thing might happen this time.

As the pace of the campaign quickened, Buford's popularity increased. Talk that he would be the next sheriff circulated in the county. Pauline, just out of bed after her battle with hepatitis, came home from the beauty shop one evening in an enthusiastic mood.

"Honey, everyone is saying you'll win the sheriff's race hands down," she said and kissed him. "I'm so proud of you, I don't know what to do. I knew you'd win."

"Don't count the votes before they get into the ballot box," Buford warned. "You never know about people. Sometimes they change their minds overnight."

"There's too much favorable talk about you for that to happen," Pauline insisted. "Like the old saying, 'where there's smoke, there's fire.' "

Louise Hathcock had also heard the rumors of a Pusser victory and immediately sent word to Buford that she had a six hundred dollar campaign gift waiting for him. All he had to do was stop by the Shamrock Motel and pick it up. Buford wouldn't even consider taking her money. He hated Louise and everything she stood for. Her latest exploit had been the killing of her husband, Jack, on May 22, 1964. A McNairy County Grand Jury had no-billed her after she had claimed, "It was him or me." Pusser was convinced that she'd murdered Jack simply to get him out of her way.

The state-line operators began to focus more and more attention on the McNairy County sheriff's race. As Pusser's popularity increased, the operators on the line became more restless and worried.

The campaign went smoothly until two weeks before the August election date. Then Sheriff Dickey, barely forty years old, was found dead in his wrecked car beside U. S. Highway 45 near the state line. Speculation that Dickey had met death at the hands of the state-line hoods ripped through the county. Many people believed that the criminals, confident of a Pusser victory and afraid Dickey's knowledge of their activities might be used against them, had arranged the "accident." However, nothing to substantiate the foul play theory was ever uncovered by county and state officials during an investigation of the mishap.

In spite of Dickey's death, a large number of voters cast ballots for him, and for a while, it was uncertain whether Dickey or Pusser would pull the most votes. However, when the election sheets were all tallied, Pusser had three hundred more votes than the dead sheriff had received, and for the first time that anyone could remember, many traditionally Democratic communities went Republican.

Pauline could hardly control her excitement. "I told you that you'd win," she boasted, hugging Buford. "I knew it all the time."

"I knew it, too," said Carl Pusser. "I told Buford a long time ago that folks around here were sick and tired of the law allowing things to go on like they have been at the line."

Buford gently pushed back from his wife.

"Well, like I promised in my campaign, I'm going to clean out that bunch of crooks over there," the newly-elected sheriff said. "And I'm going to start the day I take office."

With the certainty of more money coming in, Buford moved his family out of the trailer and into a three bedroom house. There, the children had more room to entertain their friends. There was a nice yard and a patio. Pauline was especially pleased with the kitchen. "Now, more than one person at a time can get in it," she said, laughing.

On September 1, 1964, Buford Pusser was sworn in as McNairy County sheriff, and at age twenty-six, he became one of Tennessee's youngest sheriffs. As a one-man police force, Buford kept his word and began the task of corralling the county's lawbreakers. His father was his only deputy, and Carl's major job was tending the jail.

Buford began making regular routine checks of the roadhouses and state-line joints. Although a chair over the head and a few cuts and bruises were often his rewards for a night's work, he continued making the rounds and arresting lawbreakers.

The White Iris, owned by Carl Douglas "Towhead" White, an ex-convict, and the Shamrock Motel, operated by Louise Hathcock, caused Pusser the most trouble. The White Iris featured dancing, bootleg whiskey and beer drinking. Call girls, one-hour rooms with a special price tag, illegal whiskey and beer to go were the main attractions at the motel. Towhead and Louise had become intimate friends since the death of her husband.

White, knowing that Pusser made the rounds of the beer joints by himself, often tried to bluff the sheriff by making threatening remarks. However, he made sure that he had two or three of his "punks" within earshot before popping off to Pusser.

One night, the sheriff decided to play White's game. He parked his car in front of the White Iris and sat there in his sheriff's uniform listening to country music on the radio. Several would-be customers slowed, then drove on when they saw Pusser. After about an hour, White stormed out of the club.

"Look, Pusser. Find some other goddamned place to loaf. You're not welcome here!"

Pusser cocked his sawed-off shotgun, which was lying in his lap.

"I'm just protecting your property, White. It's my duty, since you're one of our taxpayers."

"Don't do me any favors, Pusser. I can protect my own property. I don't need a tin-horn sheriff like you to do it."

Pusser shoved the shotgun out the car window and aimed it straight at White.

"I've had enough of your lip. Get inside and close

this rat joint down. Right now! Or I'll padlock the door and take all your asses to jail."

Seeing that the sheriff meant business, White quickly complied. He didn't want to take a chance on losing his beer license, and he knew that Pusser could get help simply by reaching for his two-way police microphone.

*   *   *

Early one morning in November 1964, the headlights of Pusser's car outlined a man walking along U. S. 45 near Selmer. Frost lay heavy on the landscape, turning the red clay hills and black bottomlands to silver under a full moon. The air was brisk and calm.

The hitchhiker, young, slender, and wearing a thin coat, stood erect with his right thumb in the air as Pusser's unmarked sheriff's car approached. Buford stopped to let the young man in, planning to give him a warm jail bed, a hot breakfast, and send him on his way. He never got the chance. As soon as he got in the car, the hiker pulled a switch-blade knife from his coat pocket and drove it twice into Buford's chest. While the blood drenched Buford's sheriff's uniform, turning it a dull red, the hiker leaped out of the car and ran into the darkness.

Buford drove himself to the McNairy County Hospital, where doctors patched his wounds and then held him twenty-four hours for observation. He had tasted violence for the second time; he still carried the scars from the state-line beating in 1957.

Although he shrugged off the stabbing as something that might happen "once in a lifetime," Pauline didn't share his feelings.

"Honey, you need to be more careful when you deal with strangers," she advised. "You've got to learn to stop trusting people so much. I'm real worried about you. I'm afraid you're going to get killed."

Buford, who was sitting on the living room couch, stood up. He stared out the window into the yard.

"You worry too much, Pauline. The knife wounds aren't that serious. I only had to spend one night in the hospital, and I'm practically as good as new right now."

"No, you're not. You're weak and you need to rest. Please, honey, for the children's sake and mine, promise me you'll be more careful."

"Don't worry, everything is going to be all right."

Buford's assailant was never apprehended, and he theorized that the hitchhiker was a "wanted man" who had panicked when he realized that he had crawled into a car with a lawman.

Less than a month after the stabbing, Pusser was called to a rural house fire, where two persons were trapped. He waited until fireman had extinguished the flames, then helped rescue workers remove the charred bodies of the victims. The house had burned so quickly that there had been no hope of getting them out. As he started to leave, he noticed an old model Dodge parked a short distance from the smoldering ruins. The rear of the vehicle was almost touching the ground. In the car's front seat, the faces of a Negro man and woman were illuminated by the light atop a fire truck.

Pusser walked up on the left side of the car where the man sat slouched under the steering wheel.

"What's in the trunk of your car?" he asked.

The man, frightened by Pusser's voice, quickly straightened up in the seat.

"Nothin', man. Just the usual junk. You know. Tire, jack, tools and stuff like that."

Pusser shook the car from side to side and he heard a sloshing sound from the trunk. "That stuff back there must be made of water instead of iron and metal from the way it sounds," the sheriff said. "Open up the trunk."

Pusser walked out in front of the faded gray Dodge for a look at the license plate numbers while he waited for the man to get out and open the trunk. The man instead started the car and accelerated forward. Pusser leaped and landed spread-eagle on the hood. He held onto a radio aerial with his left hand while he reached through the side window and tried to snatch the keys from the ignition.

"Stop this damned car! Stop it, you crazy fool," Pusser yelled.

The driver didn't answer, but took a knife from his coat pocket and stabbed Pusser five times while the woman leaned over and slammed a pipe wrench against the sheriff's head. Pusser slumped from the hood of the speeding car and sprawled backwards onto the gravel road.

Several persons who witnessed the incident ran to Pusser, who was already trying to get up.

"Lay down and take it easy, Buford," a man said. "Don't try to get up. You took a nasty fall."

"I don't see why he wasn't killed," said another.

"Oh, my God!" cried an elderly woman. "Look at his back. He's been stabbed and he's bleeding like a stuck hog."

Buford was taken to the McNairy County Memorial Hospital. The attackers' car was found abandoned two miles from the scene of the fire with thirty-one gallons of "white whiskey" in the trunk. The license plates were found to be stolen, and the identity of the couple was never discovered. Buford, however, recovered with remarkable speed and returned to his job in less than two weeks.

Pauline had encouraged her husband to run for sheriff, but now she regretted it. He had been in office only a few months and had already been stabbed seven times. She remembered her words about the lack of danger on the job. When Buford had first gone into police work, she'd said, "Nothing to do but arrest a few drunks and speeders." She had sure missed it that time, she thought, but she knew Buford well enough to know that he would never resign from his job, so she didn't nag him about quitting. Instead, she worried and fretted in silence.

*   *   *

It soon became evident to Buford that if he were to be able to clean up the county as he had promised, he would have to have full-time help. He worked the area between the sheriff's office and the county court-room as if he were prospecting for gold. He wanted a deputy, but the magistrates always said, "No money." As in most Tennessee counties, elected magistrates controlled the financial outlays for public services. Dickey had used part-time deputies—farmers, busi-nessmen, and loggers—but Buford believed that a sheriff's department should have a full-time staff cap-able of handling trouble quickly, not a group which required hours and innumerable telephone calls to round up.

Moreover, public opinion was beginning to get behind the idea of enlarging the department. "This damned county ain't progressed one iota in the last hundred years," one old-timer complained after hear-ing that the magistrates had refused to hire a deputy sheriff.

"The way this county is growing," the man added, "one man can't handle this law business by himself. But they ain't never been any paid deputies, and you can bet they ain't gonna start having any now."

Buford, however, was convinced that the county court would find some funds in the near future, but until that time, he would have to find a new money source to hire a full-time deputy sheriff. An odd twist of fate finally produced the help he needed.

About a month after his last appeal to the court for help, an informant told Buford about a truck parked in Selmer and loaded with whiskey. Since McNairy County was dry and it was illegal to sell or possess any kind of liquor except beer, the sheriff immediately investigated the tip.

Buford found one hundred and fifty cases of taxed whiskey in the canvas-covered truck bed and confiscated both the truck and the whiskey. Later, the vehicle and booze were sold at a state auction, and the county received $5,200 for its share of the profits. The county court used a portion of the money to set up a special sheriff's account at the bank. It was the first time in McNairy County history that the sheriff's department had been authorized to have an account of its own.

Four months after Pusser took office, the squires granted his request for a full-time deputy. Buford hired Jim Moffett, a close friend, who lived near Adamsville. Moffett, of medium-build and in his early thirties, was a quiet man with a deceptive personality. He appeared to be an easygoing individual who would let anybody push him around, but Jim Moffett could be just as tough as he was good.

Pusser and Moffett began hitting the honky-tonks and state-line dives hard. They usually picked up a carload of drunks or bootleg whiskey on every trip. A visit to the Shamrock Motel always netted several

cases of taxed whiskey and several gallons of moonshine, as well as a tongue-lashing from Louise Hathcock. The officers would take her to jail, but she
always managed to pay her fine or post bond before
spending any time behind bars.

Buford Pusser also waged a war on the illegal
whiskey-makers and gave Moffett orders to spend
some time in the woods looking for stills. Just before
Christmas in 1964, Moffett sighted a moonshine
operation in a clump of trees surrounded by open
fields. He drove back to Selmer and informed Pusser about the still.

"It's located in an ideal spot," Moffett told the
sheriff. "It'll be hard as hell to slip up on them with
all the open fields around."

"Well, maybe we can flush them out into the open
if we can't get up to the still site," Pusser said. "We'll
check on it tomorrow."

Late the next day, Pusser and Moffett crawled on
their hands and knees to the still through a field of
waist-high Johnson grass. Three men were standing
several feet from the still. The sheriff and his deputy
scanned the fields for signs of life, then eyed the
hundred-pound sack of Domino sugar on which all
three rested a foot.

"They're carrying sugar to the still so they won't
leave any truck tire tracks across the field," Buford
whispered.

"Pretty smart idea," Moffett smiled.

"Yeah—but it can run into a lot of hard work."
He laughed under his breath.

The smallest of the three men left his partners and walked toward the patch of woods. Pusser and Moffett slipped around to the opposite side of the woods and into the area where the still was located. They could no longer see any of the men. Then the slender moonshiner approached the still, and Pusser stepped out in front of him and whispered, "Shhhhh. Just sit down and be quiet."

The stunned man obeyed. Pusser whistled a quail call, and in a few seconds the other two whiskey-makers walked into the trap.

"I'll be a son of a bitch," one of the men said to Pusser. "I thought that was an all-clear signal. It's got where a man can't believe his own damned ears anymore."

Pusser and Moffett laughed.

"Now, I guess you boys are going to tell us that this moonshine still ain't yours," Pusser predicted.

"Hell, no, we ain't gonna tell you that," replied the first man who was caught. "You law dogs caught us red-handed, and we'll take our medicine like full-grown men."

Both Pusser and Moffett were surprised by the man's remarks, but they didn't show it.

"I appreciate your attitude," the sheriff replied. "Makes my job a lot easier this way."

"Hell, man, we ain't mad at you. We knew we was

takin' a chance when we started makin' this wildcat whiskey. So we lost."

Pusser made the men promise to be in his office the Monday after Christmas, then sent them home. He confiscated three gallons of corn liquor and dynamited the still along with two barrels of mash.

The sheriff seldom got rough with the moonshiners. He treated them fairly and usually accepted their word for bail bond. He knew where all of them lived, and if they failed to show for trial, he arrested them and showed them little mercy.

During Buford Pusser's first year as sheriff, he raided forty-two illicit whiskey stills and arrested more than seventy-five moonshiners. With the county till healthy from the sale of illegal whiskey and confiscated vehicles, the squires authorized Pusser to employ a second deputy. Petie Plunk, short, stocky, in his mid-forties, joined the Pusser forces. Plunk was even-tempered and gifted with a happy-go-lucky personality.

The state-line raids increased, and heat generated by Pusser began to take its toll. Many of the weekend honky-tonkers found other places to throw their "private parties" and the figures on cash register receipts dropped.

Louise Hathcock decided it was time to make Buford Pusser another business offer, and one night when he walked into the motel, she called him aside and slipped five-hundred dollars into his pants pocket.

"That much is yours every month if you'll leave us alone," she promised.

Pusser slowly fingered the money out of his pocket and then let the bills fall to the floor.

"I've told you before, Louise, that I don't want your goddamned money. You can't buy me off. Period."

"Look, Buford. I know you're pissed-off about that trial in Corinth that time, but you shouldn't hold it against me for what my niece and nephew done to you."

"I don't give a damn who was responsible for that trial. You state-line whores and cutthroats are all the same in my books. Two peas in a pod. And sooner or later I'm going to run all your asses out of my county," he threatened, storming out the door.

Pusser started to get into his car, then decided to check around the motel before he left. A few feet away in one of the rooms he heard a man and woman arguing.

"Look, you bitch. I gave you twenty-five dollars to be with you all night. One time and now you're already harping about having to go home."

"What do you mean, one time?" she snapped.

"I don't give a damn. The deal was for all night. And you're going to keep your part of the bargain if I have to tie you spread-eagled to the bed."

Pusser stopped outside the motel door.

"All right. This is the sheriff. What's going on in there?"

"Nothing, sheriff. Just having a little discussion with my husband," came the meek reply.

"What do you mean *husband?* Does he always pay you twenty-five bucks to go to bed with you?"

The woman hesitated.

"Oh, no, sheriff. You misunderstood us. Didn't he, honey?"

The man mumbled something to the effect that everything was all right.

Pusser knew he couldn't file charges against the whore unless the man would sign the warrant, and he could tell he wasn't going to do that. Many of the male customers were married businessmen who did not want the publicity of a trial.

The sheriff went back to his car and got a flashlight, then made his way behind the motel. There he found a new Cadillac and a 1962 pickup truck, which appeared to have nothing in it but several empty burlap bags. However, a closer inspection revealed eighteen gallons of moonshine.

Pusser summoned Louise Hathcock and ordered her to open the trunk of the Cadillac. Two cases of taxed whiskey were found in it. He confiscated the Cadillac and pickup along with the whiskey and arrested Louise. As she had done countless times before, however, she posted bond.

A week later, Louise made Pusser an offer of one-thousand dollars per month to let the Shamrock operate with a free hand.

"I told you, Louise, that I don't want your damned

blood money," Pusser said sharply. "If you mention payoffs to me again, I'm going to file charges against you for attempting to bribe an officer."

Louise Hathcock made no more efforts to have an under-the-table deal with Buford Pusser.

The state-line rackets were not the only problems the sheriff had to cope with. Early in 1965 he began receiving complaints from local citizens concerning the Tennessee State Troopers' practice of forcing accident victims to use one wrecker service. According to the complaints, the troopers assigned to McNairy County were calling Bob Hertz at Selmer to tow all wrecked vehicles, regardless of whether or not the owners wanted it. Pusser told Highway Patrol Captain Noah Allen Robinson, who was in charge of the McNairy County area, that he wanted the troopers to begin rotating the wrecker business instead of giving it all to one company.

"Let Hertz finish out this week, then start giving all the other wrecker firms an equal share of the business," Pusser told Robinson.

"The best way is to set each wrecker company up on a weekly call basis, then rotate them every week," he added.

Robinson made no comment.

The next week, Pusser heard a 10-45 call over his two-way police radio. The numbers meant that there had been a traffic accident with no injuries. Out of curiosity, he drove to the scene of the accident on U.S. 64 and found there had been a minor, two-car collision. He also found a Hertz wrecker there. He charged out of his car toward the state trooper.

"What in hell is going on here?" he yelled. "I told your troopers to rotate these wreckers! Hertz is not towing either one of these cars in!"

Then he added: "This damned shakedown racket is going to stop in my county. I know you boys are getting payoffs for throwing all the wrecker business to Hertz. But as of right now, the racket is over."

The sheriff waited until another company's wrecker arrived, then left.

The following weekend, the troopers set up roadblocks in McNairy County and hauled thirty-three persons to the Selmer Jail. Captain Robinson ordered Carl Pusser to lock all of them up for drunkenness.

Seconds later, Buford walked into the overcrowded office.

"What's going on here?"

Robinson was sitting on the edge of Carl's gray metal desk. He had all the characteristics of a tough, movie-world cop. "Sheriff, I want all these people locked up for drunkenness. Also, some of 'em are facing charges of driving while intoxicated," he said.

Briefly, Pusser glanced from one face to the other.

"They don't look drunk to me."

"But, sheriff, you're not the judge," the captain snapped.

"That's right. However, I'm going to call Judge Treece right now and see what he thinks about this deal you're trying to pull."

The sheriff went back to his private office and telephoned General Sessions Judge Clyde Treece and asked him to come to the jail. Within a short time, Treece arrived. He was a polite, mild-mannered man. Judge Treece talked to the "prisoners" and then held a private conference with Buford.

"It's my opinion, sheriff, that only two of those persons out there are drunk enough to lock up," he said.

"Your opinion is good enough for me."

Pusser went back into the jail office, ordered the two drunks to stand to one side, then told the rest of the people to go home.

"Wait just a damned minute," Robinson interrupted. "These are my prisoners, sheriff, not yours. If you won't lock them up, I'll take them to Hardeman County and put 'em in the Bolivar jail."

"You know better than that, Robinson. You can't take them out of McNairy County. You arrested them here, and this is where they have to be jailed and tried.

"Judge Treece says there are two of them who are drunk enough to lock up. So I'm going to lock those two up, and the rest can go home."

Pusser led the two men into the elevator and pushed the third-floor jail button. Robinson hopped in before the door closed. There was absolute silence during the elevator ride. The sheriff jailed the two men, ignoring Robinson, and again got on the elevator. Robinson followed him.

"Look, Pusser. You got no authority to turn my

prisoners loose," the state patrol captain said. "And I don't like it a damned bit."

Suddenly, Pusser grabbed the front of Robinson's uniform and shoved him against the side of the elevator wall.

"Listen, Robinson, don't mess with me, or I'll lock your goddamned ass up in jail and call the governor and tell him where you're at," Pusser threatened. "Do you understand me? Do you? You might push other folks around, but you aren't pushing me," Pusser said, turning Robinson loose.

Buford trembled with anger.

When the elevator reached the bottom floor, Robinson wasted little time in leaving the sheriff's office.

A week after Buford Pusser's argument with Robinson, Tennessee Safety Commissioner Greg O'Rear drove from his Nashville office to McNairy County for a talk with the sheriff and Adamsville Mayor Leonard Blanton. Blanton, a prominent West Tennessee politician and a successful businessman, had asked O'Rear to come to Adamsville after hearing about Pusser's run-in with the troopers. After the meeting, O'Rear said that a new group of state troopers would be assigned to McNairy County and some of the old ones would be fired.

The commissioner kept his word.

*   *   *

As the end of Buford Pusser's first two-year term

neared, he announced his candidacy for reelection. This time, however, his wife would not support him. Pauline Pusser pleaded with Buford to give up the idea of running for sheriff again. She wanted him to settle down to an ordinary life.

"Honey, I don't want to nag you, but please don't run again. It's too dangerous. I've spent too many sleepless nights already," she said.

"I told you, Pauline, that you worry too much about nothing," he answered. "I love you and want you to be happy, but you must realize that I have a job and an obligation to fulfill. Please, try to understand that this is something I have to do."

Pauline knew that Buford's mind was set and there was nothing she or anyone else could do to change it. He had pledged not only to local citizens, but to himself, that he was going to clean up the state line, and no man was any better than his word, according to Buford.

Clifford Coleman, a Democrat who had been sheriff before James Dickey, was Pusser's major opponent in the campaign. The 1966 McNairy County sheriff's race, however, commanded little attention, and Pusser defeated Coleman by a three-to-one margin.

McNairy Countians were well satisfied with the job Buford Pusser had done during his two years in office. He had kept his campaign promise; had hit the state-line dives hard and had refused to be "bought off" by anyone. Honest citizens were convinced that

Buford would put the hoodlums completely out of business, or go to an early grave trying.

*   *   *

Louise Hathcock nosed her late-model car off U.S. 64 into the parking lot designated for customers of Fred's Place. The nightspot, located two miles east of Adamsville in Hardin County, was owned by Fred Plunk.

Large black letters on the white-washed block building told travelers on U.S. 64 that the club featured smoked hickory pit barbecue, cold beer, dancing, and a weekend band.

Louise entered the club through a back door and found an empty stool at the bar. She ordered a can of malt liquor, then asked the whereabouts of Plunk.

"Fred will be back in a minute. He just stepped over to the house for a few seconds," the bartender said. Plunk lived within walking distance of the club.

Louise had known Plunk for several years, and she liked him. He was her kind of man—easy to get along with.

"Give me another one," Louise told the bartender as she emptied the can quickly. "You have to drink a case of this damned stuff to even get a small kick."

Plunk strolled through the door. He was short, in his mid-fifties with thin, gray-flecked red hair. Plunk's patience was his greatest asset.

"Well, Louise Hathcock! What in the hell brings you over here?" he asked.

"I thought maybe I'd come over and get drunk. But I can't do it on this weak-ass malt liquor," she laughed.

"I think I can remedy that," Plunk replied, turning and walking into a back room.

He came back carrying a fifth of bourbon.

"Put this behind the bar and get us a couple of glasses and some ice and Coke," Plunk told the bartender. "And you'd better set two cans of beer in front of us just in case the law comes in. If the cops drop by, we'll just be sipping beer."

Plunk and Louise talked, danced and drank whiskey and Coke until closing time. Then for no apparent reason, she suddenly drank a toast to her dead husband.

"Here's to Jack Hathcock, the son of a bitch. He's in his grave where he belongs, and in hell, too!"

Plunk made no comment. When Louise was drunk, it was better not to say anything.

Louise Hathcock didn't know it at the time, but a grave awaited her, too, and the wait was not going to be long.

CHAPTER VIII

"Mrs. Hathcock is Dead, Ain't She?"

It was February 1, 1966, 10:15 in the morning, and Buford Pusser was on his way to arrest Louise Hathcock. Approaching the Shamrock Motel, he slowed the police cruiser as Jim Moffett shifted restlessly beside him. Petie Plunk fumbled with his wide-brimmed hat in the back seat. Plunk read the sign in front of the motel outloud: "Television, Tile Baths, Carpeting, Pool, and Air Conditioning. Package Beer To Go. They left out bourbon," he muttered. Pusser whipped the car off U.S. 45 into the driveway of the Shamrock and hopped out with Moffett and Plunk at his heels. He had two warrants in his pocket, one for theft, the other for possession of whiskey, both to be served on Louise Hathcock.

A young couple, who had been standing in the shadow of the motel, hurried toward Pusser and the deputies.

"Which one of you is the sheriff?" asked the wiry, sandy-haired man.

"I am. What's the trouble?"

"We're the ones who called you about the robbery."

The sheriff was surprised to find the complainants at the motel. He had expected them to drive up after he arrived.

"My wife and me were robbed of one hundred and twenty-five dollars by Mrs. Hathcock," the young man said. He kept glancing toward the main office, which was less than a hundred feet away.

"We've been here a couple of days. Then about an hour ago, we decided to head back to Illinois, so I went to the office to pay our tab."

His wife, a petite blonde barely out of her teens, interrupted: "Honey, you'd better not tell them. Let's forget the whole thing and go home. You know what that woman said."

"I'm not worried now that the sheriff and his men are here," her husband said.

"That's right, ma'am. Don't worry about the woman in the motel there. She's not going to hurt you," Pusser promised.

"Well, when I went to pay our bill, Mrs. Hathcock noticed the amount of money I had in my wallet, so she told me to empty it on the counter top. At first, I thought she was kidding. Then I realized she wasn't when a couple of big goons walked up beside her."

Again he glanced nervously toward the office.

"She told me that I wouldn't get hurt if I'd just quietly put my wife in the car and drive back to Illinois. She warned me that if I called the law, my

wife and I would both end up in the Tennessee River
with a concrete block tied around our necks."

"Louise Hathcock wasn't kiddin'," Pusser said.
"She's mean as a barrel of rattlesnakes. A lot of other
people she robbed *did* wind up in the river."

The blond shuddered and moved closer to her husband.

"I told you, honey, we should have left when she
told us to. I'm scared to death!"

The girl was close to having hysterics, Buford
thought. Neither one of them should have been in this
place, but being from out of town, they couldn't know.

"Now, you heard what the sheriff here said. He'll
handle things, so don't worry. Everything is going to
be all right."

Pusser asked the young man to sign the theft warrant, then he and the deputies entered the motel office.

Louise Hathcock was sitting at a small desk behind
the registration counter examining a set of receipt
books. She was wearing a white duster and a pair of
red house shoes. A glass nearly full of bourbon and
Coke rested on the edge of the desk.

She looked up, an expression of surprise on her
face. She had not seen the sheriff and his men arrive.

"Got a warrant for your arrest, Louise. You've
been charged with robbing a man and his wife of one
hundred and twenty five dollars."

"Who signed the warrant?"

Pusser had asked the couple to wait in his car while
he served the warrant.

"An Illinois man says you clipped him out of his money."

"That's a crock of shit! I ain't clipped a soul out of anything. Where's the son of a bitch at? He won't tell me that to my face!"

Louise Hathcock's face was flushed. It was obvious to Buford that she had been drinking heavily. She probably hadn't stopped from the night before, he thought.

"I'm not going to argue with you, Louise," Pusser said firmly. "You've been charged with robbery and you're under arrest. You're going to jail and that's that."

Pusser moved back from the counter.

"Keep an eye on her, boys, while I look around for some booze."

Moffett ordered Louise from behind the reception counter into a cushioned leather chair near the window. He wanted her where he and Plunk could keep a close watch on her movements.

"Look, Moffett," she slurred. "I didn't rob that man and woman of a single penny. They're damned liars, both of 'em!"

"No use to talk to me about it," Moffett replied. "The sheriff is the boss."

"Yeah, I know. Big bad Buford Pusser. He thinks this is Dodge City and he's Matt Dillon," Louise remarked.

Pusser returned in a few minutes carrying a half-case of Yellow Stone whiskey.

"I'm also charging you with illegal possession of liquor in a dry county."

Louise stood up.

"Now listen, sheriff. I can explain this whole situation. Let's go to my private office where we can talk without interruption."

"We can talk right here."

"No, I got some things to tell you that are confidential. I'm going to level with you about the whole operation. I want to talk to you alone."

"Okay, but make it snappy. I ain't got all day."

"Let me get my drink. I need something to calm my nerves," Louise said, walking to the desk and picking up the glass in her left hand.

Pusser opened the office door, ordered Louise to walk out first, then followed close behind. The motel madam's private office was in Room Number One, located just around the corner. Louise toyed with a ring of keys, finally found the right one, and unlocked the door. Pusser was surprised at the neatness of the room. Hangers of cleaned clothes in cellophane bags hung on the inside door handle. A green-quilted spread on a double bed matched the curtains and carpet. Across from the bed was a polished maple dresser, its top arranged with tubes of lipstick, powder boxes, and hair curlers. An oak desk, with a small reading lamp on it, sat in a far corner.

Louise pushed the door shut, but the clothes caught between the lock and the catch, and the door crept open. Slowly, she slid her right hand into her duster pocket, withdrew a .38-caliber pistol and pointed it at Pusser. She still held the mixed drink in her left hand.

"God damn you, you're not taking me anywhere!"

Pusser jumped back, striking the edge of the door as Louise fired. The impact from the collision with the door knocked him across the bed, and the stray bullet plowed plaster from the wall.

She dropped the glass of whiskey to the floor and ran to the bed. Aiming the pistol directly at Buford's head, she squeezed the trigger again. The click of the hammer hitting the shell in the chamber sounded like a cannon's roar.

Pusser, sprawled across the bed, unholstered his .41-caliber magnum and fired at her. The bullet caught Louise in the left shoulder and spun her around. The second shot struck under her right arm, tearing a hole through her heart and lung. Blood spurted onto a curtain as Louise Hathcock grabbed her chest with both hands, then slumped to the floor with a slowness that fascinated Buford. He could not take his eyes away. For a moment he watched the blood flow from the wound in her side, then holstered his magnum.

When they heard the shots, Moffett and Plunk hurried into the room. The deputies were almost shocked to find the sheriff still breathing. They had been sure that Louise had led Buford into a trap and murdered him.

"You all right, Buford?" they asked in unison.

"Yeah, fine. But I wouldn't have been if her gun hadn't misfired. Don't move the body or touch anything until the Tennessee Bureau of Investigation checks the place," Pusser said, leaving the room.

In the reception office, Buford telephoned his father at the jail and told him what had happened. "Call the TBI and an ambulance," he said.

Buford cradled the phone and stared blankly at a wire rack of picture postcards near the counter. He was numb with the mere fact of being alive. If the gun had gone off—but he didn't even want to think about it.

An old man who had been hanging around the Shamrock for years came into the office and slouched down in a chair. His unshaven face was white and he trembled uncontrollably.

"Mrs. Hath—Hathcock is—is dead, ain't she?"

Pusser didn't answer.

The old man's faded blue eyes fell on the whiskey case.

"Please, sheriff. I need a drink real bad!"

Pusser didn't argue the point but dug a half-pint out of the cardboard case and handed it to the man. Hands shaking, the old derelict held the bottle to his lips and drained the contents in one steady swallow. For a moment, Pusser, too, thought about downing one of the bottles. He needed to wash away the memories of this terrible day—this day on which he had been forced to take his first human life. He could still see, at that very second, the blank, distorted look on

Louise Hathcock's face as she fell dead on the floor, and he wondered if he would ever be able to erase that look from his mind.

After TBI agents had inspected the scene of the shooting, Louise Hathcock's body was taken to the Memorial Hospital in Selmer and then to the Shackleford Funeral Home. Medical tests showed that she had 24.8 percent alcohol in her blood, much more than enough to indicate intoxication.

The body was later transferred to a Corinth, Mississippi, mortuary, and Louise Hathcock was buried with simple ceremonies in West Point, Mississippi.

District Attorney Will T. Abernathy of Selmer, after checking the TBI reports of the Hathcock shooting, felt that Buford Pusser had killed the woman in self-defense. However, the DA presented the case to the McNairy County Grand Jury for official action. The grand jury wasted little time in ruling that Louise Hathcock's killing was justifiable homicide, and the case was closed.

The case was considered closed by law officials, but not by the hoodlums who frequented the Shamrock, White Iris and other state-line joints. Rumors circulated that a "price" had been put on Buford Pusser's head, and in mid July, after the motel shootout, an anonymous telephone call was made to the sheriff's office in Selmer.

Carl Pusser snuffed out a filter-tipped cigarette in an ashtray on the dispatcher's desk, then lifted the telephone receiver.

"Sheriff's office."

"Who is this?" a man's voice asked on the other end.

"Carl Pusser."

"Listen, you old gray-haired bastard—and listen good. There's a $10,000 reward on you and Buford's head, and I'm going to collect it!"

"Go ahead and collect it, you son of a bitch, if you think you're man enough," Carl replied angrily, slamming down the receiver.

The elderly Pusser didn't take the telephone threat seriously. Someone was always calling and boasting of what they were going to do to Buford, or to him. But the threatening calls increased in number and frequency at the jail, and Pauline began to get similar calls at the Pusser home in Adamsville.

"We're going to take your kids out in the swamps and cut off their sweet little heads. That way, the swamp water will get a little coloring," one caller told Pauline.

"Your husband ain't got long to live. There's a $10,000 reward on his head, and I'm going to collect it. He's going to die just like Louise Hathcock did— with a lot of bullets in him," another caller said.

Although they were both upset and worried, Buford and Pauline didn't know what they could do about the calls—except wait.

*   *   *

On the night of January 2, 1967, Buford Pusser
was driving on U.S. 45 north of the state line when
a new Chrysler with two male occupants passed him
at a high rate of speed. He immediately gave chase,
reaching speeds up to ninety-miles-per-hour before
getting the car stopped about a mile from the
Tennessee-Mississippi line.

Pusser approached the car from the left side. Suddenly, the driver drew a .25-caliber automatic and
began firing. Two bullets struck Pusser in the left
cheek, one ripped into his left forearm and another
grazed his abdomen. While he staggered to his car, the
Chrysler sped away, but Pusser was eventually able to
drive himself to the McNairy County Hospital.

Meanwhile, the FBI from the Jackson, Mississippi,
office launched a search in the area for Carl Douglas
"Towhead" White and Julius Oliver French. Less than
a month before the incident both men had escaped
from the federal prison at Maxwell Air Base in Montgomery, Alabama, where they were serving time for
whiskey violations. The two men were prime suspects
in the shooting of Buford Pusser.

White, whose mother lived in Corinth, had been
involved in state-line activities for years. He had also
been a close friend of Louise Hathcock.

Three days after the Pusser shooting, White and
French turned themselves in to authorities in Mont-
gomery. The pair was never officially linked to the
Pusser incident, but most law officers in the Selmer-
Corinth area, including Sheriff Pusser, believed that

White and French had been involved in the shooting.

*   *   *

Pauline Pusser was never the same after the highway shooting of her husband. Although Buford recovered successfully, the terrifying thought of having to view his bullet-riddled body on a cold mortuary slab continually ran through her mind.

Pauline was close to her husband's work, cooking meals for the inmates and handling most of the dispatching duties at the sheriff's office. She often found some consolation in talking with the Reverend E. E. Thomas when he held religious services for the prisoners at the jail. Thomas, pastor of the United Pentecostal Church in Adamsville, was always able to lift her spirits, at least temporarily.

"Sheriff Pusser is a good man, Pauline. The Lord is not going to let some criminal snuff out his life," he told her. "Remember, David, too, had a tough battle with Goliath, but he won because God was on his side.

"Sheriff Pusser is a lot like David. The only difference is that the sheriff has many Goliaths to fight while David had only one. The sheriff will win because God is with him," the Reverend Thomas assured her.

"I hope you are right, Brother Thomas," she said. "I don't know what in the world I'd do if something happened to Buford. I don't think I could stand it."

CHAPTER IX

"Buford Pusser's Got to Die"

An old drunk named Bill sat in a Corinth honky-tonk, ordered another beer, and talked with his friends. "You can bet one thing," he said over a new glass of beer. "Towhead White will blow Buford Pusser's head off for what he did to Louise Hathcock."

"Yep, Tow and Louise were close as two peanuts in a shell," the drunk's friend, John, agreed. "Even while he was in the pen, she took care of his business for him."

A woman with long, stringy brown hair, eyed a small sausage pizza on the bar in front of her, then joined in the conversation.

"I knew Louise Hathcock real well. She was a good ole gal. That damned Pusser had no right to shoot her down like a common dog."

"Yore right Maxine," Bill said. "Pusser is a low-down, sorry son of a bitch."

The woman tore off a piece of the pizza with her fingers.

"You want my pocket knife, Maxine?" John asked.

"Hell, no. No tellin' what you've been doing with it all day. I don't want that nasty thing around my vittles," the woman sneered.

Everybody laughed.

"White'll break out of Leavenworth—just wait and see," Bill continued. "He'll break out and blow Buford Pusser to hell."

"That's right. Ole Tow has been known to bust out before," John added. "Remember that time when they claimed him and that other feller shot Pusser near the state line. He'd just busted out of the federal joint at Montgomery that time."

"I wouldn't give two cents for Pusser's life right now. If Towhead don't shoot him, he'll have it done," the woman said, wolfing down the last of the pizza.

After Louise Hathcock's death, similar conversations took place in one beer joint after another along the state line. Word had spread that Carl Douglas "Towhead" White had marked Buford Pusser for death. White apparently had vowed to avenge the killing of his old girl friend. At the time, White was serving a three-year federal prison sentence at Leavenworth, Kansas, for participating in a three-state moonshine whiskey ring.

No one, however, including police authorities, doubted White's ability to have "outside" connections do the job. Born in Sumner, Mississippi, White had decided at an early age that he wanted to be the "Al Capone of Alcorn County." Now at age thirty-three, in the Al Capone mold, he was the undisputed king of the Mississippi-Tennessee state-line operations. The Federal Bureau of Investigation kept an active file on him, which included criminal activities in at least ten states, and his police record was as thick as the New York telephone directory. He had also maintained close ties with organized crime elements all over the South. A word from White, behind bars or out, could get a person killed.

On the other hand, although White often got into trouble, he also had a knack for talking his way out of it. He had a smooth tongue and likeable ways. His slender, six-foot-two frame, soft brown eyes, innocent grin and low, earnest voice worked to his advantage with women and other men. He could laugh and joke one minute and then, with only his eyes showing the change, turn to solid granite the next. People did just about anything he asked them to do. Those who knew him best said he could have become anything he wanted to be.

What he wanted to be, apparently, was one of the top hoods in the southern part of the United States. A state-line motel was his headquarters, and he always came back to the Shamrock and Louise.

Now she was dead—shot by the Tennessee sheriff who had taken it upon himself to put Towhead and his gang out of business.

In his Leavenworth cell, White swore that Pusser wouldn't go unpunished. He told friends who visited him that Pusser wasn't "long for this world," and no one doubted that he meant what he said.

White had first gotten into trouble with the law when he was only sixteen. He had robbed a Corinth supermarket, received a stiff reprimand, and been turned loose.

In August 1954, White was arrested by the FBI in Butte, Montana, and charged as a "deserter-fugitive" from the army. FBI records show that White joined the Air Force in 1952 and the next year entered the army, enlisting both times at Jackson, Mississippi. Later, military officials ousted him from the service with a dishonorable discharge.

From Butte on, Carl Douglas "Towhead" White's face became known to policemen and sheriffs in cities across the country. He collected a string of arrests stretching from Montana to Mississippi on charges ranging from public drunkenness to burglary.

In March 1956, White was arrested in Corinth for being intoxicated on the street. In June he was held as a material witness in a burglary in Gretna, Louisiana. In July he was arrested in Columbus, Mississippi, for jury tampering. Authorities said White tried to buy off a juror in a burglary trial in which one of his close associates was involved. However, the charges failed to stick.

In December, police in Clarksdale, Mississippi picked him up for investigation. In June 1957, White was lodged in the El Paso, Texas, jail for hitch-hiking. Two days later, U.S. Marshals slapped him with a warrant from Quitman County, Mississippi, charging unlawful flight to avoid prosecution.

In September 1957, he hit the "big time." He was locked behind the heavy doors of the Mississippi State Penitentiary at Parchman. A Quitman County jury convicted him on two counts of burglary and sentenced him to two years on one count and three on the other, but he was paroled before the first term was served.

Memphis, Tennessee, officers arrested him in November 1961 on a warrant from Mississippi charging parole violation. The next month Memphis police again got him on the same charge and in January he was sent back to Parchman to finish his burglary sentences.

Free again in 1962, White ran afoul of the law in Kenosha, Wisconsin, and in December, Memphis authorities nailed him on a fugitive warrant from Wisconsin charging White with burglary. He beat the rap.

Early in 1963 the sheriff at Gulfport, Mississippi, picked him up for investigation and vagrancy. In October of that year, officers in Baton Rouge, Louisiana, took him into custody for investigation of burglary and vagrancy.

In 1965, White made the top of the list of the "Ten Most Wanted" criminals in Texas. He was said to be a close friend of a man held in Texarkana jail in connection with a trailer park robbery and murder in

Covington, Louisiana. Once again, White escaped conviction.

His luck, however, ran out in September, 1965, when he became active in a moonshine whiskey racket which spread over a three-state area. A federal jury found him guilty of transporting untaxed liquor and sentenced him to the Leavenworth prison.

Now, according to reliable reports, White was plotting the death of the sheriff who had dared to meddle with his kingdom and his woman.

CHAPTER X

The Twelfth of August

Pauline nervously slipped into a pair of dark brown slacks, a white blouse, and black loafers while Buford put on his tan sheriff's uniform. It was 4:30 in the morning, August 12, 1967. Minutes before, an anonymous caller had told the sheriff "serious trouble was brewing on the stateline," and Buford had said he would be right there. For some reason, however, Pauline felt particularly upset over this call, and she insisted on going with her husband to answer the complaint. She did not want Buford to go to the state line alone again. Although she knew she could do little or nothing to help if they ran into trouble, at least she would be with him. She wouldn't be pacing the bedroom floor at home, worrying, waiting for the phone to ring. Now, with the two of them in the front seat, the late-model Plymouth sped out of Adamsville at ninety-five miles per hour, heading west on U.S. 64.

"Wonder what the trouble is all about at the line?"

Pauline asked, shoving a cartridge into a stereo tape recorder under the dash.

"I don't know. The guy on the phone said they were having some bad trouble on New Hope Road. He said if they were gone when I got there, to go on up to Hollis Jordan's beer joint. Probably a bunch of drunks trying to shoot each other."

The sounds of country music vibrated softly from a rear speaker.

"Well, I hope it isn't anything serious," Pauline said.

Buford turned off U.S. 64 onto the black-topped Gilcreast-Stantonville Road which stretched six miles to Highway 57.

"Have you got everything ready for us to leave tomorrow?" he asked.

"Yes. All but a few odds and ends. Are we going to leave early?"

"I thought we'd try to be on the road by seven, if that's all right with you."

"That's fine. I'll sure be glad to see Mom and Dad again. It's been a long time."

Buford and Pauline were looking forward to a family reunion with Pauline's parents, Mr. and Mrs. Jack Mullins, in Haysi, Virginia the following day. Pauline's sisters, Mrs. Cathy Wright and Mrs. Aileen Brown, both of Chicago; her brothers, Griffin and Clayton Mullins, both of Louisville, Kentucky; and their families, were all going to be there.

Buford slowed, then turned right onto Highway 57. It was only five more miles to New Hope Road. New

Hope Road was a shortcut from Adamsville to U.S. 45 and the state line. The rough, narrow strip of pavement was approximately seven miles long.

Pusser touched the brakes and Pauline grabbed a door handle as the car whipped onto New Hope Road. The sheriff glanced at the automatic shotgun next to his right knee. Out of instinct, he felt for the holstered .41-magnum pistol on his side.

The car sped past the small New Hope community where farmers were already in the barns feeding and milking cows. In the east, redness was creeping into a cloudless sky. The woods along the road were alive with early morning sounds.

"This is going to be a beautiful day," Pauline commented. "Makes you want to live forever."

Buford didn't answer. He kept his eyes on the road ahead where he expected to see trouble at any moment. In their concentration, neither he nor Pauline saw or heard the long, black car approaching from behind.

"We ought to be getting close to the spot where the trouble is supposed to be," Buford said, and frowned, turning the steering wheel to dodge a large hole in the road.

"Yes, or maybe they've already gone up to Jordan's Tavern," Pauline said.

"Yeah, that's more than likely what they've done. Damn. I wish the county would fix this road. It's like a washboard."

Suddenly, Buford and Pauline heard the roar of an engine and the black car was beside them. Orange flames belched from a .30-caliber carbine, and the window on the left side shattered, spraying Pusser's face with slivers of glass. The shots missed him and slammed into Pauline's head.

She moaned, grabbing Buford's arm as she slumped down in the seat. Buford floor-boarded the Plymouth. His only thought was escape. He had to get help for Pauline.

He knew that he didn't have a chance against the assailants in the semi-darkness with Pauline dying beside him. The two guns he had in the trunk were useless to him. Besides, he hadn't even been able to use the automatic shotgun or the magnum he had in front with him.

Pauline—he had to get help for Pauline.

Buford drove two miles down the road and skidded to a stop, thinking that he had escaped the assassins. Gently, he placed his wife's head in his lap. When he saw the gaping hole in her head, he was nearly sick with fright and rage.

"Oh, God, please don't let her die! Please, God, don't let her die!" he prayed aloud.

Then the black car came by again. This time, a volley of shots riddled the car at point-blank range. Buford caught two slugs in the lower jaw, and his whole chin dropped to his chest, held only by a flap of skin. He sank to the floorboard, as another bullet ripped through the metal car door and shattered Pauline's skull. Blood soaked the seat, floorboard and occupants.

The ambushers left, thinking Pusser and his wife dead. When he was sure that they were not coming back, Buford gripped the steering wheel and pulled himself up into the seat. He looked at Pauline and knew at once that she was dead. For the first time in his life, he felt completely helpless. The bastards had failed in their efforts to destroy him physically, he thought, but they had succeeded in destroying the most vital part of his life by killing Pauline.

Although he was critically wounded, Buford placed his hand on his wife's warm cheek and promised to avenge her murder.

"I love you, Pauline. Only God knows how much I love you. They'll pay for what they've done to you. This I promise," he mumbled.

Pusser drove until he reached U.S. 45 and pulled into the driveway of an abandoned grocery store. He tried to lift the microphone of his police radio, but it kept slipping from his blood-smeared hands. He heard a vehicle stop, and looked up. The driver of a bread truck stared at the bullet-riddled car, then quickly drove away.

Buford wiped his left hand on the back of a dry pants leg, then picked up the mike. He pushed the transmitter button and his incoherent message wobbled over the air waves to various sheriff's dispatchers in the area.

He wondered why he couldn't talk. When he looked in the rear view mirror, he knew.

He realized only then that his chin had been blown off.

The only dispatcher who recognized Buford's voice was his father. Carl was busy cooking breakfast for the prisoners in the jail in the McNairy County Courthouse when he heard the message. The only word Carl could understand was "45". He immediately thought of U.S. 45 and the state line.

Then the telephone rang, and Carl was told by Albert Kitty, a grocery store owner near the line, that a state trooper had been killed at an old store at New Hope Road and U.S. 45.

Kitty, seeing Buford slumped over against the door with his tan sheriff's uniform on, had assumed that the officer was a highway patrolman.

"That ain't no trooper—that's Buford. And he's still alive but he's badly hurt. I just heard him trying to call in on the radio. I'll talk to you later, Al, I've got to get him some help."

Carl sent the message about Buford out on both the state and county police radios.

State Trooper J. R. Reed was the first officer to reach Buford Pusser. He saw that Pauline was dead and that the sheriff was hurt too seriously to talk about the shooting, so he made him as comfortable as possible and waited for an ambulance.

Selmer Police Chief Hugh Kirkpatrick arrived shortly after Reed, followed by an army of law enforcement officers from the area.

"Pusser's had it this time," remarked one policeman.

"His whole face is blown apart. He'll be lucky to live until they get him to the hospital."

"Yeah, he'll never make it," replied another. "His wife is already dead. That car looks like it's been through the Vietnam War. Wonder who the dirty sonsabitches are who did this?"

"Some of that state-line bunch. They've been after Buford for a long time. Looks like they finally got him."

Carl Pusser assigned the breakfast-serving chores to a trusty and called his wife.

"Something bad has happened to Buford. Get to the hospital as quick as you can."

"Oh, no. What happened?"

"I don't know any details yet. Just get on out to the hospital!"

Helen Pusser started to telephone Pauline and tell her the bad news, but then she decided to let someone else break it to her. She knew how upset Pauline had been lately about Buford's safety. Helen had no idea that Pauline had been murdered in the front seat of her son's car. She had talked to her at home only last night.

"Please, dear God, if it be Your will, spare Buford's life," Mrs. Pusser prayed as she began dressing for the trip to the hospital.

Carl was waiting outside the emergency room when the ambulance screeched to a halt, and Buford was pulled out on a stretcher. He looked at his son's distorted and bloody face and cursed to himself. He lit a cigarette and leaned against the side of the ambulance. He didn't think his son would live. Half of his face had been blown away. "The dirty, rotten sonsofbitches finally got him," he mumbled to himself. "They finally got him!"

Joe Ebb Wyatt, manager of the Shackleford Funeral Home in Selmer, drove up in another ambulance and got out.

"Hi, Carl. I'm real sorry about what happened this morning."

Carl didn't answer.

"What do you want me to do with the body?" Wyatt asked.

"What body?"

"Pauline is dead."

The words hit Carl Pusser like a giant fist in the face. He was stunned. He thought Pauline was at home. Slowly, he walked to the rear of the ambulance and opened the door. He gazed for a moment at the form under the white sheet.

"The bastards had no right to kill her. She never harmed a hair on anybody's head in her life," he said. Then he paused and added bitterly:

"Whoever did this called me at the jail about 2:30 this morning. He wanted me to send Buford out to the New Hope Road, said they was having a lot of trouble out there.

"But the man never would tell me what kind of trouble it was. The information was too sketchy—so

I didn't call Buford. I guess the sonsofbitches called him later at the house."

Carl moved closer to the sheet-covered stretcher.

Wyatt gently placed a hand on Carl's shoulder.

"Don't look at her, now, please. Wait until we fix her up. It will be much easier on you." Then he looked at the other stretcher.

"No, Joe Ebb, I want to see for myself what they done to her," Carl said, slowly pulling back the sheet.

"The dirty low-down bastards. The rotten sonsabitches."

He turned away. Pauline had been almost like a daughter. What was Buford going to do without her— if he lived. And the kids. What about the kids?

"Take her on to the funeral home, Joe Ebb. We'll be down later." Carl turned and walked toward the emergency room door.

Helen Pusser arrived before Carl reached his destination.

"Is Buford all right? How bad is he hurt?" Helen asked.

"I don't know yet. The doctor's still got him in the emergency room. Pauline was with him. She's dead."

Helen Pusser's slender face froze with disbelief. She, too, had thought Pauline was at home.

Pauline! How come she was with him? How did it happen?"

Carl watched the ambulance carrying Pauline's body leave the hospital driveway and turn onto U.S. 64 toward Selmer.

"Some damned thugs ambushed them early this morning on New Hope Road. They nearly blew Pauline's head off. Buford is seriously shot."

"Is he going to live?"

"I don't know."

Although Helen Pusser's heart was heavy with grief, she was too stunned to cry. The tears would come later. She entered the emergency room office where a nurse asked her to wait while she summoned Dr. Harry Peeler. Dr. Peeler asked Helen not to look at Buford.

"It would be much better if you waited until later," he said. "I'm going to transfer him to Memphis and you can see him just before he leaves."

"No. I want to see him now. Is he going to live?"

"I think so."

Helen followed Peeler into the room where her son lay on a blood-soaked sheet atop a narrow table. He was bare to the waist. A nurse had just covered the lower part of his face with a towel-like cloth. An orderly checked a bottle of blood hanging over-head.

"Get another bottle. Keep the transfusions going," Peeler snapped.

"Buford's in terrible shape, isn't he doctor?" Helen asked.

"Well, things could be worse. His chin has been torn apart by bullets, and he's lost a lot of blood. But I think he'll pull through."

Helen moved close to the table and placed her

hand on Buford's forearm. Buford, who had never lost consciousness, blinked his eyes.

"Just rest, son. God will take care of you. I have faith that everything is going to be all right."

Dr. Peeler ordered Buford transferred to the Baptist Hospital in Memphis where a team of specialists was waiting to try to save his life. Shelby County officers, fearing the assassins might return to finish their job, also were preparing to guard his hospital door around-the-clock.

Carl and Helen Pusser, however, remained in Selmer to tell Buford's and Pauline's children about the tragedy.

"We've got to tell the kids right away," Helen told Carl, "and I don't want to be the one who tells them."

"I don't either."

"Somebody's got to do it," said Deputy Petie Plunk, who was standing nearby. "If you like, I'll tell them."

"We'd appreciate it, Petie," Carl replied. "Me and Helen have been through too much already. We'll ride along, but you break the news to the kids."

It was almost ten o'clock when Plunk and the Pussers arrived at Buford's modest brown-shingled house in Adamsville. The three quietly entered the dwelling. Helen Pusser felt the presence of Pauline. It was only last night that she had been here with her in this very room—had talked and enjoyed their close relationship. Now, it seemed impossible that Pauline was dead.

Plunk made his way to a back bedroom. All three of

Diane, Buford's step-daughter.

Mike and Dwana.

the children were still asleep. Plunk stood and looked at them for a minute. This was going to be the hardest job he had ever had to do. He didn't even know how to begin.

The deputy shook the youngsters one at a time. "Wake up, kids, wake up."

Gradually, they awoke, and Plunk waited for them to rub the sleep from their eyes before speaking. Then the words came out in a rush.

"Children—it's hard for me to have to tell you this, but your mother is dead. She was killed early this morning in a shooting on New Hope Road. Your father was also seriously hurt. He's in the hospital in Memphis."

Mike, a slender, handsome youth with his mother's features, broke into sobs. Diane, who also bore Pauline's looks, stared at Plunk with disbelief for a moment, then she too, cried. It took several minutes before Dwana grasped what had happened. Then she cried louder than the rest. At the time, Diane was sixteen; Mike twelve; and Dwana, six.

*   *   *

A few hours after the ambush, rumors circulated in McNairy County that Buford Pusser had murdered his wife and shot himself to cover up the crime. The talk was worse in area beer joints.

"Buford Pusser just killed his wife and shot himself," an elderly man announced loudly, hurrying into Fred's Place through a back door.

Fred Plunk, who was busy cleaning up his dance hall after a wild night, looked up.

"Buford Pusser done what?"

"Shot his wife right through the head, then shot himself to make it look good," the man repeated.

"When did all this happen?"

"About daylight this morning on New Hope Road. Buford's in a Memphis hospital right now. He had to make it look like an ambush."

"Bullshit!" Plunk said disgustedly. "I don't believe a damn word of it. Buford Pusser didn't shoot his wife anymore than you did. Him and Pauline were a fool about each other. Have you and the rumor-toters come up with a reason for him wanting to shoot his wife yet?"

The old man didn't answer.

"If I was you, I wouldn't be spreading anymore talk like that around," Plunk added.

Authorities who investigated the shooting said evidence proved beyond a doubt that Buford Pusser could not have engineered the crime. TBI agents, McNairy County sheriff's deputies, FBI and other peace officers of the area inspected the ambush scenes and found fourteen empty .30-caliber cartridge cases. The bullets used in the attack, it was learned, all contained soft-nosed, lead slugs. Chief Deputy Sheriff Jim Moffett and a TBI agent examined Pusser's Plymouth and found eleven bullet holes in it. The investigators concluded that the ambush was motivated by Buford Pusser's campaign to clean up the illegal activities on the state line. The shooting of Louise

Hathcock was also mentioned and Towhead White's name was brought into the picture.

The officers launched a full-scale search for the assassins, and Paul Johnson, governor of Mississippi, ordered his state's highway patrol to aid in the investigation, since the murder and shooting had occurred close to the state line.

Tennessee Governor Buford Ellington, at the request of District Attorney General Will T. Abernathy, offered a $5,000 reward for information leading to the arrest and conviction of the slayers. Bill Smith, owner of Walgreen's Drug Store in Selmer, headed a fund drive to raise additional reward money. Smith's efforts netted $2,500.

Today, the $7,500 is still gathering dust.

*   *   *

Mr. and Mrs. Jack Mullins had wanted to take their daughter back to Virginia for burial in a cemetery on a mountainside overlooking their home, but Buford had said no. He wanted his wife buried in Adamsville. Pauline's parents seemed content after learning of his feelings.

Buford Pusser had also instructed his mother on the amount of money to spend for the funeral.

"After you reach a certain price range, you pay for things you don't get," he told her.

Buford felt bitter about the funeral business. He

had worked around mortuaries for several months and had often said: "They all make a tremendous amount of profit. There is a big mark-up on caskets and everything."

The funeral services took place in the Church of Christ in Adamsville. The blue metal casket bearing Pauline's body rested in the front of the church on a carriage hidden by a ruffled, matching skirt. The casket was covered with arrangements of flowers tagged with notes of sympathy. There were approximately three hundred saddened people in the church, the front pews reserved for members of the immediate family. Outside, hundreds of other mourners stood to show their respect for Pauline and her husband. Only the sobs of Dwana Pusser pierced the quiet of the sanctuary.

Inside the church, Helen Pusser glanced at the casket, then at members of Pauline's family who sat near her. She had tried to handle everything the way Buford had wanted it. She had already made two special trips to Baptist Hospital in Memphis for the purpose of checking with him about arrangements. Little Dwana had helped her select Pauline's coffin.

The service, conducted by Lindsey Garner, minister of the Adamsville Church of Christ, and the Rev. E. E. Thomas, a Pentacostal minister, was simple and effective. The choir sang two hymns, one of them requested by little Dwana, and Garner read from the one hundred and twenty-first Psalm, his voice strong and confident in the little church.

Rev. Thomas, who had comforted Pauline many times, stood behind the rostrum. His voice, which usually had a fiery ring to it, this day was calm, almost soft.

"Due to this thing that has happened to our friend, neighbor, companion, and public servant, I regret the necessity of this service today with all the feeling that I have.

"I became acquainted with Pauline Pusser during my many visits to the McNairy County Jail to see prisoners. On many occasions, Pauline expressed a fear for her husband's life, but never a fear for her own safety.

"I feel that Buford and these children are the greatest losers. Although all of us have lost, they surely have lost the most.

"There must be concern and prayer for our sheriff—the man who stands between us, you and I, all the people, and the forces which would destroy us."

Thomas hesitated a moment and then held up a news clipping from the Memphis *Commercial Appeal*.

"The headline says: 'Sheriff Bears Marks of Bravery.' I agree wholeheartedly. He does, even now, and for as long as he lives, bear those marks, those scars which are left on his body.

"And his precious wife paid the supreme price for bravery. She did not have to go on Saturday morning with the sheriff of our county. No law in the book required that she do that.

"She went beyond, and may I say far beyond, the

call of duty. And even though there was danger, which she knew, it did not stop her from being at the side of one that meant more to her than life itself.

"I do not know who is responsible for Pauline's death and the wounding of Buford. If I did, I would give the information to the proper authorities, and I urge all of you to do the same."

Thomas stepped from behind the rostrum and walked to the edge of the platform.

"I would say to McNairy County—to every citizen—that if there is one shred of evidence, it should be presented without fear, regardless of the price."

The choir began singing "Sweet Hour of Prayer," as the half-lid of the casket was raised. Hundreds, including those outside, filed past the coffin.

Pauline Pusser, lying on the white shirred satin, appeared to have merely fallen asleep. She was attractive in the light blue dress with the dark flowers and high neck. And the wig, which covered the bullet holes, looked like her natural hair.

That day she was buried in red clay on a hillside beneath two small oak trees in the Adamsville Cemetery.

CHAPTER XI

"The Ballad of Buford Pusser"

Eighteen days after the slaying, Buford Pusser came home.

Although Dr. Rufus Cravens, a plastic surgeon from Memphis, had worked long on his face, cutting, stitching, wiring bones and teeth, it remained scarred and broken.

The doctor said Pusser's face had been struck by at least two bullets and possibly three.

Helen Pusser tried to tell Buford about his wife's funeral and told him that James Hall, an Adamsville postal worker, had taped the services. But Buford didn't want to hear the tape nor any details of the funeral. He was still in a vacuum of bitterness and disbelief.

His only comment about Pauline's funeral arrangements came after he received an invoice for the wig.

"The beauty operator said we could have the wig for seventy-five dollars," he said. "Then when we

Helen Pusser

get the bill, it turns out to cost one hundred and twenty-five dollars, a nice profit of fifty bucks.

"That's what you call real friends. Pauline had her hair fixed there all the time."

Helen Pusser stared for a moment through the living room window at two young boys riding bicycles down the street.

"Well, it isn't right, Buford. But it's over now, so we might as well try to forget it."

Buford remained silent. People were all alike, he thought, always trying to make a buck, even if it meant taking advantage of a dead friend.

Buford recovered quickly, despite the severity of his wounds, and the doctors marveled. He immediately began looking for clues that might lead to his wife's killers.

The sheriff was sure that Towhead White had master-minded the murder, even though it was not possible for him to have been the actual trigger man. White was still behind federal prison bars at Leavenworth, but Buford was convinced that Towhead had arranged the "contract" for the slaying.

Pusser traced his first suspect to Boston, but before he could gather enough evidence to justify an arrest, the man was shot to death in gangland style near Boston Harbor. There were other suspects, and Buford had no intention of giving up.

After the New Hope Road shooting, Pusser changed his style of dress. Instead of his usual tan sheriff's uniforms, he wore tailored suits, colorful ties, and immaculate white shirts, thinking that he would be less noticeable in street clothes.

He also traded cars often, seldom driving the same one for more than a month. Townspeople had a hard time keeping up with the color or model of automobile the sheriff was driving from one day to the next, and that was the way he wanted it.

Buford armed himself to meet any situation. He replaced the automatic 12-gauge shotgun with an AR-

15, similar to the M-16 used by American soldiers in Vietnam. He retired his old .41-caliber magnum to a trophy case and holstered a new .357 magnum.

Buford Pusser was finally frightened. He lived daily in the shadow of fear—fear that the gunmen would return to finish the job they had only half done on the morning of August 12, 1967. He became suspicious to the point of obsession, taking no chances and trusting no one outside a small circle of relatives and intimate friends.

One sunny afternoon, for example, a West Tennessee newspaperman dropped by the sheriff's office for a feature story. Pusser, always friendly with members of the press, suggested they talk business over a catfish dinner at his favorite restaurant. The newsman quickly agreed.

Pusser and the reporter climbed into the sheriff's new Ford XL and headed for Shaw's Restaurant, located near Shiloh National Park, scene of one of the Civil War's most famous battles. Buford claimed that Shaw's had the best catfish and hushpuppies in the State of Tennessee.

He slowed for a set of railroad tracks south of town, then braked for a traffic light.

"Want a drink?" the sheriff asked.

"Yeah. I wouldn't mind a little something to wash this McNairy County dust out of my throat," the reporter said.

"Reach behind the seat there. You'll find a couple

of bottles in a paper sack. Vodka and gin. Take your pick."

The newsman selected gin, as Pusser whipped into a service station, opened the car door and got out.

"You want 7-Up or Coke?"

"7-Up."

Pusser returned with two paper cups of 7-Up and handed one to his guest. The reporter started to twist the cap, but the sheriff grabbed the bottle.

"Let me see it! Has it been opened?"

Pusser examined the seal closely, then twisted the cap off. He sniffed the bottle several times. The newsman was puzzled.

"You can't ever tell," Pusser said. "Those sons of bitches might have switched bottles and left me one with poison in it. I didn't have the car locked."

The journalist understood. A man who has had his face half blown off by shotgun blasts and watched his wife die right beside him had to be suspicious of everything, he thought.

The reporter poured himself a healthy drink, stirred it with his finger, then took a deep swallow.

"Tastes fine."

Pusser spilled gin into his cup and stirred it with a ball point pen. He downed it in two swallows.

The sheriff drove fast, speeding by Joplin, Axel, Pebble, and Acton, all crossroad communities of Mc-Nairy County, on the nineteen-mile trip to Shaw's Restaurant. At the restaurant, he introduced the newsman to Eddie and Bob Shaw, owners of the establishment.

"You're with a fellow now who can eat his weight in catfish and hushpuppies," Eddie Shaw told the reporter.

"We always put on two orders when we see him walk in. It's a waste of time if you don't get Buford Pusser started with at least two orders."

Everyone laughed.

After downing a few drinks of gin and soda, Pusser proceeded to eat several orders of catfish and hushpuppies.

Enroute back to Selmer, Pusser pulled into a service station to use the restroom. He entered the restroom and bumped into a well-dressed man who was washing his hands in the sink.

"Excuse me, sir," Pusser apologized.

"Ah, hell, that's all right, buddy. Don't worry about it. Say, you want a little nip of bourbon? Just happen to have some on me," the man said, laughing and taking a half-pint bottle of Old Charter out of his back pocket.

"Got to be careful, though," he continued. "This is a dry county. We don't want the law to nab us."

Pusser grinned.

"Thanks just the same but I'll pass this time. I'd be careful with that stuff around here. Like you said, it's a dry county."

"Don't worry. I've heard about that mean-ass sheriff they've got here. I sure don't want to tangle with him."

Pusser laughed and walked out the door. He knew that the tourist trade brought a lot of money into the area, and unless an individual was drunk and disorderly, he rarely arrested anyone for taking a drink.

*   *   *

Buford Pusser, like his mother, seldom displayed his emotions, but instead kept his thoughts and feelings locked inside.

After Pauline's death, he often became depressed and moody—alone, as he had been before he met her. Sometimes he went to the cemetery where he stood among the sun-bleached flowers and rain-spotted ribbons surrounding her grave. He would stare at the large double headstone with the chiseled letters: PUSSER and search for an answer to his wife's death. Why had her life been taken? he asked himself. She was innocent of any wrongdoing, a kind, precious woman, he thought.

At other times, he was haunted by the face of Louise Hathcock. He could still see the blank stare in her eyes after he had shot her. He could see the blood pouring like a waterfall from the hole in her side. Why had he been forced to kill her? Being a lawman was no easy job—not in many ways, he thought. The memory of her death lay heavy on him; though he knew that he had been justified, he could not erase the fact that he had killed her.

Buford tried to forget past tragedies by keeping himself occupied with other things. He spent long hours with his daughter and stepchildren. Often he would put on a white apron and barbecue ribs or steaks on a grill in the backyard.

Buford was thankful for his close relationship with the children. After their mother's death, Mike and Diane had chosen to live with him rather than their father, and he felt good about their choice.

When Diane grew a little older, however, she and Buford encountered trouble when she began wanting to stay out late with her friends. He demanded that she be home at a reasonable hour every night, and Diane didn't like the rule. Finally she moved to Memphis, but only after having written several hundred dollars worth of checks on Buford's account. A few weeks later, Buford heard that she had married a young man from Jackson, Tennessee, but the marriage did not last. Not long after the wedding, Diane left her husband while he slept one night. Buford felt that he had failed with her somehow. He couldn't seem to stem her almost uncontrollable urge for parties, no matter how much he talked to her. If Pauline had been alive, she could have helped Diane, he thought. She could have done something about the wildness and unrest. None of it would have happened, but Pauline was dead.

*   *   *

The sheriff's morale was boosted somewhat one day when Eddie Bond, a singer from Memphis, stopped by the McNairy County Courthouse for a visit.

Pusser was outside the courthouse talking to a couple of farmers when Bond drove up in a Cadillac and got out. The singer immediately recognized Buford from newspaper pictures and walked toward him.

"Hello, Sheriff Pusser. I'm Eddie Bond."

"Hi, Eddie. I'm real pleased to meet you."

"Thank you, Sheriff. Boy, I've heard a lot about you. It sure is an honor to meet you in person."

"The feeling is mutual," Pusser said, grinning shyly. "Come on down to my office."

The sheriff had heard of Eddie Bond for several years. The thirty-seven-year-old country music singer had a Saturday afternoon television show on Channel 13 in Memphis and a daily program on KWAM Radio. Pusser had occasionally watched Bond's TV show and had often tuned him in on the car radio. The Memphis television and radio stations covered a wide area of West Tennessee, including McNairy County.

Bond had been a regular performer for three years on the Louisiana Hayride in Shreveport and had been a guest star of the Grand Ole Opry in Nashville and the Big D Jamboree in Dallas, Texas. In 1954, he was voted "Mr. DJ USA" by WSM Radio in Nashville. His first release on Mercury Records entitled "Rocking Daddy" had been a top seller. Now, he owned a

Pusser (left) with Eddie Bond.

private recording company in Memphis called TAB Records.

The sheriff's office was in the basement of the four-story courthouse. The office was air-conditioned and had a black-flecked tile floor and two-tone brownish walls. A large colored photograph of Dwana hung next to the door. White curtains dotted with purple flowers covered the one row of windows. A green metal desk and a filing cabinet were in the center of the office and an orange couch was in a far corner.

"Sit down, Eddie, and make yourself at home," the sheriff said as he slid into a swivel chair behind his desk.

"Rather stand, sheriff. I need to grow a little taller. I been eatin' a lot of turnip greens and drinkin' a lot of fresh buttermilk but it hasn't helped a bit," Bond joked.

Pusser laughed.

The entertainer had the kind of personality which made it easy for him to make friends. Within a short time, Eddie could make a person feel as if he had known him all his life.

Bond chatted with Pusser several minutes before telling him the real reason he had driven the ninety miles from Memphis to Selmer.

"You know, sheriff, I been thinking," he said with the touch of a professional con artist. "Your life sure would make good material for a song to put on records. I bet it would sell a million copies."

Pusser hesitated and put his hands together as he leaned back in the swivel chair.

Bond watched the play of emotion on Pusser's scarred face.

"What do you think?" the singer asked.

"Well, I don't really know. I'm not that familiar with writing songs and making records."

"I think it would be a terrific idea," Bond quickly responded. "Of course, you would get a cut off the record sales."

Pusser stood up.

"Like I said, I'm not familiar with writing songs and all. But if you want to write a song about me, it's okay. I'll be glad to help you anyway I can."

"Great! I'll put a song together, then come back to Selmer and let you see what I've come up with."

"Okay. Like I said, I'll be glad to work with you, Eddie. Any way I can help, just let me know."

Bond, with the help of Jim Climer, a KWAM disk jockey, wrote a song entitled "Ballad of Buford Pusser."

The Memphis singer later returned to Selmer for another meeting with Pusser. The sheriff liked the ballad and gave his okay for its release. He also signed a contract with Bond and formed a company called Bond-Pusser Enterprises. A clause in the contract gave Bond exclusive rights to marketing material on the sheriff's life.

The "Ballad of Buford Pusser" was released on TAB Records and got a lot of airplay on KWAM, one of Memphis' largest country music stations, where Bond was program manager. It was also a hit on juke boxes in West Tennessee and North Mississippi honky-tonks. People liked to hear Eddie Bond sing:

> *"Well let me tell you all a story about a*
> *Two-fisted, racket-bustin' cop.*
> *Buford Pusser is the name and many years ago*
> *He vowed to put a stop*
> *To all the law-breakin', double-dealin',*
> *Under-handed crimes he knew to be,*
> *Goin' on right there in McNairy County,*
> *Tennessee."*

Several thousand copies of the record were sold. During the first two weeks, Carl Pusser peddled more than a hundred copies of the ballad at the jail for one dollar each. The McNairy County Jail became a record shop with one label in stock.

More important, for the first time since Pauline's death, Buford Pusser seemed to be returning to a normal frame of mind. He wasn't as moody or as depressed as he had been.

He had won the 1968 sheriff's race by a two-to-one margin over William Littlejohn without so much as a campaign speech, and his crack-down on stills and other illegal whiskey operations during the past four years had fattened the county treasury considerably. The new revenue had provided him with a $10,000-

a-year salary, plus expenses, and a new automobile whenever he wanted it.

Moreover, as the dives along the state line had either shut down or mysteriously burned to the ground, the criminal element there had all but vanished. And now a popular song with the sheriff as subject was enjoying attention all over the South.

Then, however, came Christmas Day, 1968. Buford received a telephone call in the sheriff's office in Selmer.

"Sheriff, this is Don Pipkins," the caller said. "Charles Hamilton's drunk out of his mind. He's over here in his apartment threatening to kill me and my wife, and he's got a loaded pistol."

"Be right there, Mr. Pipkins," Buford said. He knew Pipkins, Hamilton's cousin, owned the apartment Hamilton was living in.

Buford considered the fifty-year-old Hamilton to be a heartless killer and thought he should have been sentenced to the electric chair years ago. Hamilton had slit his mother-in-law's throat, shot a deputy sheriff, and murdered his wife. In addition to that, he had stabbed an inmate in prison and knifed another man to death in a tavern brawl. He had spent more than thirty years in prison. Now, he worked for the McNairy County Highway Department.

Buford parked his car in front of Hamilton's apartment and got out. He adjusted the .357 magnum in the holster on his side, then stepped up on the porch and knocked on Hamilton's door.

"Come in," said an overly polite voice.

As the sheriff entered the room, Hamilton began shooting his .32-caliber automatic at him. One slug streaked across Pusser's abdomen. A second whizzed past his head, and a third chipped the handle of his holstered magnum. Two more slugs slammed into the wall.

Pusser quickly unholstered his magnum and fired. The bullet smashed Hamilton between the eyes and tore through the back of his head. He had killed his second person.

The case, like the shooting of Louise Hathcock, was turned over to the McNairy County Grand Jury by District Attorney General Will T. Abernathy. As in the Hathcock slaying, the grand jury ruled that Pusser had killed in self-defense.

*   *   *

The "Ballad of Buford Pusser" continued to enjoy popularity in West Tennessee and North Mississippi. Record sales were brisk. Eddie Bond and the sheriff began to realize a profit from their business venture.

Pusser and Bond not only became close business associates, but they also became intimate friends. Buford even made Bond a deputy sheriff and presented him with a gold badge.

Later, Bond bought a 1969 Cadillac, and Pusser authorized him to equip it with blue lights, two-way

police radio and official sheriff's license plates. The
official tags bore the number "50", which was Mc-
Nairy's designated number as one of Tennessee's
ninety-five counties. Next to the numerals on the white
plates with black lettering were the words: "SHER-
IFF.'"

Pusser also authorized Bond to use his personal
call number "529" when the entertainer wanted to
use the police radio to contact other sheriff's units.

The Cadillac was registered in Buford's name because it was the only legal way Bond could equip the
car with sheriff's tags and police accessories. Pusser,
however, did not want it publicized that the Cadillac
was titled in his name. He feared that McNairy taxpayers would think they had bought the expensive
"patrol car."

Neither the sheriff nor the county taxpayers, however, had a penny invested in the $10,000 car. Eddie
Bond had purchased the Cadillac and equipped it in
police fashion himself to create a special image for
his entertainment business. The flashy black car with
the long whip aerial, blue lights, and sheriff's tags,
in fact, did draw attention every place it went.

The special favors granted Bond by Pusser were well
deserved. "The Ballad of Buford Pusser" began opening big doors for the McNairy lawman.

Mort Brisken, a Hollywood scriptwriter and television producer, heard the Pusser tune during a 30-
minute news special over the Columbia Broadcasting
System's TV network and was impressed with the

story. Brisken, who produced the TV series "Whirly Birds" and "Sheriff of Cochise," immediately pursued plans for a movie on Pusser's life.

The writer-producer flew to Memphis, rented a car and drove to Adamsville for a talk with the sheriff. After a lengthy question-and-answer session, Buford Pusser signed an agreement with Brisken giving him exclusive rights to produce a movie and television saga on his life.

Brisken informed Pusser that Bing Crosby Productions would film the motion picture and the American Broadcasting Company, the television series. Brisken collected all of Pusser's scrapbooks and headed back to Hollywood.

Three months later, Brisken mailed Pusser a copy of the movie script. The sheriff, after reading it, felt that Brisken had perhaps toned down the violence too much. Being sheriff of McNairy County had been far from glamorous, he thought, but he kept his opinions to himself.

*   *   *

Carl Pusser strolled from the jail elevator door to his small metal desk in the dispatcher's office and sat down. His devilish blue eyes glinted with anger. Carl had just had an argument with Packy Parker, a Negro trusty, who was the jail cook. Parker, who was well liked by Buford, was hard at times for Carl to

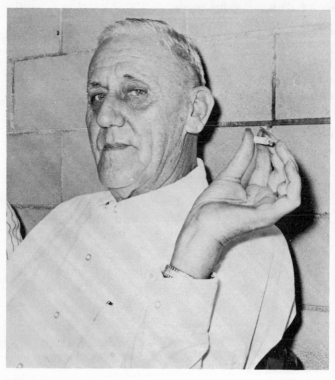

Carl Pusser, Buford's father.

handle. The elderly Pusser didn't like the trusty's arrogant attitude.

Buford came into the office, saw the angry expression on his father's face, and inquired about the trouble.

"You look madder than an ole wet hen. Who's got your dander all stirred up?"

"That goddamned Parker of yours, that's who.

He don't want to do a thing I tell him. You've got him thinkin' he ain't even a prisoner anymore!"

"Dad, be reasonable. Packy has helped out a lot," Buford said in a calm voice. "Since I started letting him cook and buy groceries, the food bill has dropped fifty dollars a week."

"I don't give a damn if it's dropped a hundred dollars a week. I ain't takin' no shit off him—especially when he's supposed to be in jail."

"I'll talk to him," Buford promised, leaving the room.

Carl knew that his son was partial to Packy Parker, but he felt that the trusty was "pulling the wool" over Buford's eyes. The sheriff had even paid expenses for Parker to fly home to Indianapolis, Indiana, to visit relatives. Buford had driven Parker to the Memphis airport to catch the airplane, then picked him up when he returned three days later.

Shortly after Carl's run-in with Parker, the trusty was released from jail. He pulled a string of robberies, however, and landed back behind bars. To Carl's relief, Parker's jailing occurred elsewhere than McNairy County.

Carl Pusser operated the county jail with an iron hand. He was fair, but stern. His word was law, except on rare occasions when Buford intervened.

The sheriff's office served as a social gathering spot for the town. People often sat around the office, chatting with Carl or each other about cotton crops, the hog market and the weather. The office was located in the courthouse basement up the hall from Buford's private office.

During thunderstorms, people, especially older folks, crowded into the courthouse basement because they feared violent weather. Most had specially-built storm cellars at their homes, but when turbulent clouds blackened the skies, they sought any underground shelter they could find. If they happened to be near Selmer at the time, they headed for the courthouse basement.

Carl didn't like having the sheriff's office used for a storm cellar or as a place to kill time, but he tolerated the situation because he knew it was good for Buford's popularity.

One evening, an old man wearing a dirty hat, clean white shirt, baggy overalls and manure-splotched plow shoes, stopped by the office.

"Hi, Carl. Is everything quiet tonight?"

"Hell yes. It's too damned quiet. I like a little excitement once in a while." Suddenly however, Carl heard an explosion of profanity from the outside. He went to investigate and found two women arguing in the street out front.

"Hey. You women cut all this goddamned cussn' and carrying on around here! I ain't gonna put up with this kind of shit. You keep raisin' hell and cussn' and I'm gonna lock your asses up in jail," Carl warned.

The women got into separate cars and left. Carl walked back into the office and had barely seated himself when a blonde woman came in.

"Carl, I'd like to see my husband for a few minutes," she asked, "if it's all right with you?"

"Well. Okay. But don't stay up there all damned night."

An old sign on the jail elevator door read: "Visiting Hours. Wednesday and Sunday. 1:00 P.M. to 4:00 P.M. Positively no admittance any other time than above." It was neither Wednesday nor Sunday nor between the hours of 1:00 P.M. and 4:00 P.M., but Carl didn't worry about that. He made his own visiting rules.

Next, Paul Moore, owner of a night club south of Selmer, came into the office and asked to see Buford.

"He ain't here, Paul. Just hang on and I'll see if I can reach him by radio."

"I'd appreciate it. I sure need to talk with him. The federal agents hit my place tonight," Moore said.

Carl contacted the sheriff and asked him to come to the office.

When Buford arrived, Moore told the sheriff that federal revenue men had raided his night spot after he had given a half-pint of gin to an agent based in McNairy County the night before.

"Royce Hodges and his girl friend came in my club last night and brought some booze with them. Then they ran out of something to drink, and Hodges asked me if I had any hard stuff he could buy. I told him I didn't have anything to sell—but that I would give him a half-pint of gin," Moore explained.

"I had a lug in the back room. You know a lug is

eight half-pints. So I gave him one. Then the next thing I knew federal agents were raiding me."

"They didn't raid you last night while Hodges was there, did they?" Buford asked.

"No, they hit me tonight."

"Where were the agents from?"

"I think they were from Jackson."

"Is the gin the only thing they got?"

"Yeah. Oh, another thing, Buford. Hodges said you was a puss-gutted sonofabitch," Moore added.

"He did? I don't know why he'd say that. I've never done anything to him."

"Well, I don't know either, but he sure said it."

"Okay, Paul. I'll check into the matter for you," Buford promised. "I don't know what I can do for you, but I'll see."

The sheriff knew the odds were against Paul Moore. The agent had caught him with gin in a dry county. Moore's intentions may have been good, but he'd have a hard time convincing a judge or jury that they were. Buford however, felt that agent Hodges, if he had done what Moore said, had been unfair. After all, Moore was only trying to help Hodges entertain his girl friend by giving him a bottle of booze.

Nonetheless, Paul Moore was found guilty of possessing gin in a dry county and fined a nominal fee.

As Royce Hodges left the courtroom following Moore's hearing, Pusser called him aside.

"I'd like to talk to you a minute down in my office."

"Sure thing, sheriff. Be right there."

Pusser went straight from the third-floor courtroom to his office in the basement. Hodges arrived before the sheriff unlocked the door.

"I'll get right to the point, Hodges. Moore said you called me a puss-gutted sonofabitch."

"That's a lie! I ain't never said a bad word about you. You know how them goddamned bootleggers are, Buford. They don't know the truth from a bunch of lies."

Hodges moved toward the door.

"Another thing, sheriff. You know you can catch them at a moonshine still, and they'll swear it doesn't even belong to 'em. Whiskey-makers are the biggest liars in the world."

"Well, I'm not going to take the word of a so-called bootlegger over the word of a federal agent. But if I knew you called me that, I'd stomp your goddamned ass right through this floor," Pusser said.

"Believe me, Buford, I didn't say it. I promise you I didn't."

The next week, Hodges apparently sought revenge against Buford Pusser. Federal agents raided Mc-Nairy County. The only whiskey-making evidence they found was the scattered debris of a dynamited still which Pusser had destroyed several weeks before.

CHAPTER XII

"I've Killed Towhead White"

It was almost midnight when Berry Smith, Jr., crossed into Mississippi on U.S. 45 and headed south for the El-Ray Motel. He was tired after several hours of driving, and he felt gloomy and uncomfortable. He wanted only to get to the El-Ray, of which he was part owner, and turn in for the night. Driving alone down the highway, feeling the warm air of spring, he could not help thinking about Shirley, his wife. He wondered where she was. They had separated two weeks before, having agreed to end their marriage, but now he wished she were with him. He wished they had never split up.

Then the red neon light of the El-Ray came into view. Smith slowed the car and turned into the graveled lot of the motel. The place was quiet, almost deserted, but there were lights on in the office. He parked his car and went inside. The door was unlocked, but no one was there.

The silence bothered him. Then he heard a car stop outside and went out the door to investigate. A middle-aged man was opening the car door.

"How are you?" the man asked, walking toward the office.

"Fine."

"I'd like to get a room."

"O.K. I've got a single halfway down. Wait a minute and I'll get the key."

"All right. Thanks."

Smith went inside to get the key, and as he walked out of the office, he heard cursing and somebody yelling at him. "Hey, Junior! You ain't got no damned business around here!"

Even before Smith saw the 1969 Chrysler parked in front of Apartment 3, he recognized the voice. Then he saw "Towhead" White slouched behind the steering wheel and next to him was his own wife, Shirley.

So that's why he couldn't find her, he thought.

White, who had been paroled from Leavenworth in January 1969, yelled again and then there was a pistol shot. Smith ducked, turned and ran to the office where he grabbed a .30-.30 rifle. Another bullet whizzed past Smith's head as he leveled the rifle at White's car. When Shirley saw the raised rifle in her husband's hands, she struggled to get the door open. When she couldn't, she took cover on the floorboard just as bullets shattered the glass. She finally got the door open, jumped out of the car, and raced toward the motel office.

Smith, crouching low, ran down the sidewalk and fired the rifle at the car again. Then he pulled a .357 magnum from his belt and emptied it into the right side of White's car.

Almost before the smoke had settled, Alcorn County Sheriff Grady Bingham had received a call at his office in Corinth about a mile away. "There's a lot of shooting going on at the El-Ray," the caller said, and hung up before the sheriff could say anything. In minutes, Bingham was at the scene.

He jumped out of his car and hurried toward the office. Smith was standing beside the bullet-riddled Chrysler.

"What's going on here, Smith?"

"I think I've killed Towhead White, sheriff. He was drunk and shot at me. He shot first."

Bingham opened the car door on the driver's side. White was slumped in the seat, blood covering his face, arms and chest. In White's right hand, the sheriff found a .38-caliber special revolver. Two bullets had been fired.

"Call an ambulance," Bingham ordered, but he knew there was no reason to hurry. Carl Douglas "Towhead" White was dead.

*   *   *

White's death on April 2, 1969, was no surprise to Buford Pusser. He had been expecting him to get a bullet in the head for a long time. The man he believed had caused Pauline's death was dead. Smith had spared him a lot of trouble, he thought. Now he could devote all his time to tracking down the actual trigger men instead of wasting his efforts building a case against White.

Pusser also believed that "Towhead" White had been behind the threatening telephone calls made to the sheriff's office and to the Pusser home before and after Pauline's murder. However, he felt he had personally settled the score with White for the threats made to Pauline.

Buford still remembered that night, the night he had almost killed "Towhead" White.

*　　*　　*

A ghostlike fog hovered in the bottomlands after an all-day rain. The night air was damp and humid. White sauntered out of the The White Iris Club and crossed Highway 45 headed for the Shamrock Motel. He was stopped by Pusser.

"Get up against the car, White, and put your hands on top," Pusser ordered, holding a .41-caliber magnum in his right hand.

"What's the idea, Pusser? You ain't got no right to do this."

"Shut your damned mouth and do as you're told before you get your head blown off."

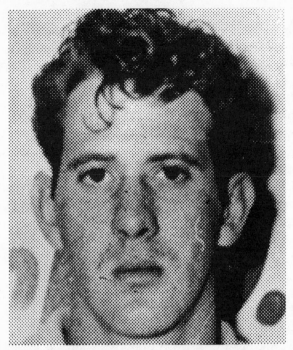

Carl Douglas ("Towhead") White

White quickly did a spread-eagle stand against the car. The sheriff searched him and found a .38-caliber pistol in a shoulder holster under his suit coat.

"This kind of hardware is illegal—but I'm sure a good law abiding citizen like you didn't know it," Pusser snapped as he slipped the pistol into his jacket pocket.

White made no comment.

Pusser handcuffed White, then ordered him into the front seat of the car.

"You ain't got no right to kidnap me like this," White protested.

"I'm not kidnapping you. I found a pistol on you and I'm holding you for investigation."

"Investigation of what?"

"Murder, threatening telephone calls, robbery— just name it, you've done it."

"Rat-shit. You ain't got a damned thing on me Pusser, and you know it."

"Look, White. You called my wife and threatened her with a lot of nasty things. You also called my father. Now you're going to pay for those calls, you low-down, filthy bastard."

"I didn't make any calls to your family. Where'd you get that idea?"

Pusser turned off U.S. 45 toward Pocahontas and the Hatchie River.

"Where you taking me, Pusser?"

"To the river. When I get through with you tonight, you won't be able to make any more telephone calls to anybody."

Fear settled on White's face.

"Sheriff, I'm telling you the honest truth. I never called your wife or father in my life. I swear."

"I wouldn't believe you on a stack of Bibles. You're a lying son of a bitch who would say anything to save your neck, but it isn't going to work with me."

Pusser whipped the car onto a gravel road. The car lights shimmered off the murky waters of the Hatchie. A coon scampered across the road and into a forest of underbrush. The sounds of frogs echoed through the trees. The area was swampy; and when the river overflowed, stagnant water stood for weeks in the bottomlands. On this night, the river was out of its banks.

Pusser stopped the car.

"Get out, White!"

"Look, sheriff. You're a man of the law. You're supposed to protect me, not murder me."

"That's a laugh. A cold-blooded killer like you talking about protection of the law. Now, get out, before I drag you out."

White slid out of the seat and stood beside the car. Realizing that Buford Pusser was almost insane with anger, he was scared.

"Please, sheriff, try to understand. I never called your family, please believe me," he begged.

"Here's the kind of understanding you need," Pusser said, slamming his fist into White's face. "Towhead" staggered back a couple of steps. The sheriff quickly followed with another punch that caught him in the mouth. The state-line boss fell in the soft mud near the edge of the water. Pusser kicked him hard in the jaw, and blood began to streak White's face. Buford cocked the magnum.

"Crawl, you son of a bitch," he said. "Crawl until your elbows and knees are out of that $200 Italian suit, and the $50 Stacy shoes are ruined."

It was hard for White to do much moving with his hands shackled, but he managed.

"I'm going to kill you, White, then throw you in the river weighted down with iron or chains—you know—the way you and Louise used to do it with all those people you robbed at the Shamrock."

White tried to raise himself up on his knees. "Please, sheriff, don't shoot me. I'm begging you," he pleaded.

Pusser laughed. This was what he had wanted. He didn't pull the trigger—that would have been too easy on White, he thought. Instead, he forced Towhead to crawl around in the muddy swamp for several hours. Then he took him back to the White Iris and dumped him out of the car. He had gotten at least some satisfaction in humiliating White and making him beg for his life. And now, somebody else had killed him.

*   *   *

Funeral services for White were held April 4, 1969, in Clarksdale, Mississippi, and he was buried in Memorial Gardens there. While White's troubles ended at the grave, troubles for those who had been associated with him were just beginning.

Berry Smith, Jr., was jailed on charges of murdering White. On April 9, he was released on $10,000 bond. Then on April 14, following a hearing, he was forced to post a $15,000 bond on the murder charge.

Smith claimed that he had been a friend of White until that night when he had had to kill him to save his own life. He told authorities that he knew of no reason why White would want to murder him.

On April 17, 1969, another White associate also found himself knee-deep in trouble. Clarksdale Police Chief Ben Collins, who was a partner with White in the juke box business, was fired by the city commissioners.

The Clarksdale Board of Commissioners voted two-to-one to fire the police chief after Commissioners W. R. Johnson and George Farris charged that Collins consorted with known criminals by entering into a business deal with "Towhead" White. The commissioners also charged him with brutality, public drunkenness and misconduct in office—using the post of chief of police to pressure businessmen into taking his juke boxes.

The Alcorn County Grand Jury, however, failed to indict Smith for murder, although it did indict him and his wife on three counts of possessing illegal whiskey for the purpose of resale. Both pleaded innocent to the charges. Alcorn County Attorney Horace Brewer later said Smith apparently had killed White in self-defense.

*   *   *

Buford Pusser, Eddie Bond and Webb Pierce arrived in Gatlinburg, Tennessee, the evening of February 21, 1970, to attend the annual Tennessee Jaycee

Eddie Bond, Buford Pusser and Webb Pierce.

convention. They checked into the Mountain View
Motel, near the foothills of the Smoky Mountains,
ate dinner, then had a round of mixed drinks in their
room.

Pusser was in Gatlinburg to receive one of the three
"Outstanding Young Men of the Year" awards from
the Jaycees. Bond and Pierce, close friends and both
avid admirers of the sheriff, had come along to help
Pusser celebrate the occasion.

The awards banquet took place the following evening. Pierce, one of the all-time country music stars,
had volunteered to sing during the entertainment por-
tion of the banquet, and he sang some of his top hits,
including "There Stands the Glass," "I Ain't Never,"
"In the Jailhouse Now" and "Wondering."

Later, as the voice of Eddie Bond singing "The

Ballad of Buford Pusser" came over the speakers around the auditorium, Buford stepped onto the stage into the spotlight and stood solemn-faced with his hands crossed in front of him. Only his eyes moved. There were three thousand people watching him.

Then the emcee, standing at a rostrum in a darkened corner of the stage, began reading from a program sheet.

"The Tennessee Jaycees tonight are proud to announce the selection of McNairy County Sheriff Buford Pusser as one of the state's outstanding young men of 1969.

"Buford, a renowned and respected sheriff, is being honored for his relentless pursuit of law and order.

"In 1969, he was made Honorary Sergeant of Arms of the Tennessee House of Representatives; received the 'Public Service' award from a national police magazine and was chosen 'National Police Officer of the Month' by the editors of a detective magazine in New York."

The emcee turned a page of his program.

"His exploits have been described in many newspapers and magazines across the country. Three ballads about his life have been recorded by Eddie Bond of Memphis.

"Sheriff Buford Pusser was county chairman of the Cerebral Palsy Fund and has served for the past two years on the West Tennessee Dignitary Panel."

"He has been wounded several times in the line of

duty. His greatest tragedy, however, was the loss of his wife in an ambush on August 12, 1967."

The emcee walked to where Pusser stood.

"On behalf of the Tennessee Jaycees, it is with great pleasure that I present you this plaque for being named one of our state's most outstanding young men of 1969."

The crowd gave him a standing ovation.

Charles A. Bell, Lebanon, and State Senator Curtis S. Pearson, Jr., Memphis, were also presented "Outstanding Young Men" awards. Bill Jenkins, of Rogersville, speaker of the Tennessee House of Representatives, was named "Pioneer of the Future."

Bell, vice president of the U.S. Jaycees, and Pearson, a car dealer and professional golfer, were both cited for their unusual civic endeavors.

*   *   *

Shortly after Pusser's selection as one of Tennessee's outstanding young men, rumors circulated that he planned to seek the governor's chair. Several Tennessee newspapers carried stories saying the colorful sheriff was planning to become a candidate for the office. The stories quoted Eddie Bond as being the major source of information. The news articles implied that Pusser would officially announce his candidacy for governor on March 26, 1970, at a Franklin County United Givers Fund benefit show in Winchester.

Eddie Bond and a number of other country music entertainers had promised to perform for the benefit. Singers from Nashville's famous "music row" included Webb Pierce, Lorene Mann, Jimmy Newman, Leon Ashley and Rusty Adams. All agreed to donate their talents to raise money for the UGF.

On the night of the show, Winchester Mayor Herman Hinshaw presented Pusser, Bond, Pierce and Miss Mann with gold keys to the city. The four, including Miss Mann, who was a Franklin County native, were organizers of the UGF event.

Halfway through the show, Pusser strolled to the microphone on the make-shift stage in the middle of the Franklin County High School gymnasium. The crowd of twelve hundred hushed. Many waited to hear the sheriff say that he had definitely decided to run for governor. Most people expected Pusser to make a long-winded political speech, but they were disappointed.

His talk was brief.

"I—I— I am very pleased to be in Winchester tonight for the United Givers Fund show. This is a very worthy cause. Money raised by the UGF goes to help many adults and youngsters who are less fortunate than most of us.

"I also want to express my appreciation for the fine hospitality shown me by Mayor Hinshaw and all the citizens of Winchester and Franklin County.

"Thank you."

Pusser walked quickly from the stage and down two

concrete block steps. A swarm of youngsters and adults hemmed in the sheriff before he could reach the dressing room. Most of them wanted his autograph, but a few wanted to talk politics.

"Sheriff, are you going to run for governor?" one man asked. Pusser hesitated while he wrote his name on a souvenir booklet.

"I don't really know at this time. I haven't given the matter any serious thought yet."

"Will you run as a Republican, Democrat or Independent?" quizzed another.

"If I should run, it would be on the Republican ticket."

"When will you make an announcement if you do decide to run?"

"Again, I can't answer the question. It depends on a lot of things." Pusser was evasive but polite, and he kept the rumors alive. He had thought about entering the governor's race and talked over the possibility with close friends and political advisors in West Tennessee. However, at no time did he map any real plans for a race to the state executive's mansion in Nashville.

Nonetheless, after the Winchester show, Pusser supporters said the sheriff wanted to make the announcement in his hometown of Adamsville and would do so on May 9, 1970, during the Adamsville Centennial celebration.

Pusser again failed to make a political speech during the Centennial event, however. He worked hard to make the celebration a success but shied away from the subject of politics. He arranged for Eddie Bond, Webb Pierce and Rusty Adams to appear on a country music show at Adamsville High School, and the show raised several hundred dollars for the Centennial group.

On May 29, 1970, during a press conference in Memphis, Buford finally said flatly that he was not a candidate for governor and announced his endorsement of State House Speaker Bill Jenkins, a Republican, who was seeking the nomination of his party.

Following the press get-together, Pusser returned to Adamsville and learned, to his surprise, that Joe Richardson, a Democratic friend, supported his Republican choice for governor.

Richardson owned the New Home Restaurant and Motel in Adamsville and followed local and state politics closely. He had great respect for Buford. Inside his restaurant, near the cash register, was one of the sheriff's "National Police Officer's" awards, which had been presented by a detective magazine. Beneath the framed certificate was an 8-by-10 autographed picture of Congressman Ray Blanton, son of a former Adamsville mayor, and although Blanton, like Richardson, was a Democrat, the Pusser award was the major topic of conversation around the New Home.

"I saw you on television today, Buford, during that Memphis press meeting," Richardson said as Pusser seated himself in the restaurant and ordered a cup of coffee after his return to Adamsville.

"I want to tell you one thing—if you're for Jenkins,

I am too, even though I'm a Democrat and he's a Republican," Richardson said.

"I appreciate that, Joe," Buford said with some surprise. Joe Richardson, he knew, was a die-hard Democrat. Previously he had voted Democratic, regardless of the circumstances.

"Yeah, Buford, I've got to stick with you. I respect your judgment on things."

"Coming from you, Joe, that's worth more than a pot of gold at the end of the rainbow."

Richardson laughed.

Pusser glanced at his watch. It was getting late, and he had promised Dwana an afternoon cook-out.

"I think Jenkins will make us a good governor," the sheriff said. "He's concerned about the people of Tennessee."

"Well, from what I've read and heard about him he seems to be a real fine man."

"He is. And I believe that he'll get the nomination. Of course, Jarman and Dunn are going to be strong contenders," Pusser said, frowning with raised eyebrows.

Maxey Jarman, a Nashville executive, Winfield Dunn, a Memphis dentist, and Jenkins were considered to be the three top Republican candidates for the nomination. Leading Democrats were John Jay Hooker, a Nashville businessman, and Stan Snodgrass, a former state senator.

"I hear John Jay Hooker is leading the race for the Democratic nomination," Richardson said.

"Yeah, I heard the same thing."

Pusser stood up.

"Well, Joe, I hate to rush off in the heat of the day like this, but I promised Dwana a cook-out this afternoon in the backyard."

"You'd better get home then. Forget the coffee, it's on me."

"Thanks. I'll make it up later."

When Pusser drove into the driveway of his home, he found Dwana wiping dust off a small Honda motorcycle he had bought her the previous Christmas. Dwana, short and chubby with shingled brown hair, ran to meet her father.

"Daddy, Mike wants to ride my motorcycle and I don't want him to. He wouldn't let me ride his— so he can't ride mine!"

"Dwana, his bike is too big for you to ride. You should share your things, especially with Mike."

Dwana, young as she was, could see that there was no use in going on with the subject.

"Are you going to barbecue this evening?"

"Yes, ma'am." Pusser grinned, walking into the house.

A one-eyed bulldog crawled out of a doghouse at the end of the driveway. A faded bumper sticker above the curved hole said: "Reelect Buford Pusser."

Dwana tossed the rag she had used to wipe off the Honda on a dust-covered saddle. Before the motorbike arrived, she had used the saddle to ride Stoney, her Shetland pony, but now Stoney rarely got out of the pasture behind the Pusser house. Dwana still loved Stoney as a pet, but the "motor age" had made him a victim of modern times.

Buford put on a white apron, dark Bermuda shorts and brown loafers. He pulled a portable grill from beneath the carport and started the charcoal burning. He enjoyed cooking, especially backyard cook-outs. Cooking was high on his list of favorite hobbies.

A bright evening sun caused every scar on his muscular body to stand out like the lines of a road map. The purple welts left by bullets and knife blades on his bare chest, arms and back reflected most of what he had to show for his nearly six years as Mc-Nairy County sheriff.

After deciding the heat was about right, Buford placed four sides of ribs on the grill. Then he watched Dwana, Mike and several neighbor kids romp through the yard playing tag.

Suddenly, for no reason that he could pinpoint, he hoped that Dwana and Mike would always be as happy as they were now and would always love and respect him. He had made a special effort to show them that he cared about them, that they were an important part of his life, and he prayed that his efforts had been successful. It was especially important to him since Pauline was gone.

Wisps of bluish smoke rose from the grill as the grease from the ribs dripped onto the charcoal.

When the ribs were almost done, Buford asked Dwana to tell Grandma Pusser to set the table.

"Okay, I'll tell Grandma," Dwana said. "Those ribs sure look good, Daddy."

"They're as good as they look. The best chef in West Tennessee cooked 'em," Buford boasted.

Dwana hurried into the house.

Pusser checked the time. Soon he would have to shower, put on a neat business suit, and go and earn the $10,000-a-year, plus expenses, that the citizens were paying him as their chief law enforcement officer.

Buford had less than three months left in the sheriff's office, and, under Tennessee law, could not seek reelection, but he still did his job with the enthusiasm of a new recruit. He didn't agree with the state law, which prohibited reelection of a sheriff who had held office for six years straight, but as in the case of taxes, he accepted it.

After supper, Pusser dressed and began his lonely night patrol which would cost the taxpayers two tanks of gasoline by the time he finished late the next morning. He stopped by the jail, found Carl chatting with an old Negro man, saw that everything was in order, and left.

"Mr. Buford sho seemed in a big hurry," the oldster said.

"Nah. He's just got a lot of patrolling to do. Got to keep an eye on things so they don't get out of hand."

Carl lit a cigarette.

"You was talkin' awhile ago about baked coon. Well, I'll tell you what's better than coon—and that's beaver."

The old Negro looked surprised.

"Beaver! Oh, Mr. Carl—youse got to be joshin' me."

"Hell, no, I ain't joking a bit. You take a beaver, soak him all night in salt water, then barbecue him and you got something that will melt in your mouth."

"Lawd. I been on this heer earth nigh on to eighty years and Ize ain't never heerd of barbecued beaver."

"Well, you don't know what you've missed until you try it. By God, it's got coon beat ten-to-one."

"I gonna try it, Mr. Carl, jest cause youse say it's good. I knows it must be."

The old Negro got out of his chair.

"I got to be goin'," he said. "I sure will try that beaver, Mr. Carl."

*   *   *

Seven men lined up at the starting gate for the 1970 sheriff's race in McNairy County. Clifford Coleman, an ex-sheriff; Wendell Hicks, a farmer; Jim Moffett, Pusser's chief deputy; Bobby Killingsworth, a singer in Eddie Bond's band; Constable R. C. Matlock; Howell Ramsey, a cook; and Alton Smith, a retired deputy sheriff were all preparing to run.

The large field of candidates not only attracted attention from prospective voters, but it caused friction among Buford and Carl Pusser and Eddie Bond.

Buford chose to back Moffett, Carl selected Hicks, and Bond endorsed Killingsworth.

"Buford, I don't know why you want to back Jim Moffett," Carl complained. "He's a renegade."

"You know damn good and well that he promised to back the nominee of the Republican committee, then when they didn't nominate him, he ran on his own. You're a Republican yourself, and you owe it to the party to stand behind its nominee."

"I can't help it," Buford said. "Jim Moffett has been with me for a long time and I'm going to support him. Besides, I think he'll make a good sheriff."

"I don't give a damn how good a sheriff he makes," Carl snapped. "You're hurting yourself by backing a renegade like Moffett."

"Regardless, I'm sticking with him."

Later, when Eddie Bond breezed into town, the scene was run through again.

"Buford, you ought to back Bobby Killingsworth. He's young like you and a good man," Bond said.

"I like Bobby Killingsworth, Eddie. I think he's a good boy, but I can't support him for sheriff. I'm going to back Jim Moffett."

"Moffett can't win."

"Killingsworth can't either. He'll be lucky to pull two-hundred votes. Besides, if he won, he couldn't serve. He lives and works in Memphis and is a resident of Shelby County."

"No. His car is registered in McNairy County and he does all his banking business here."

"That doesn't make any difference. He's still a legal resident of Shelby County."

Bond wasn't convinced. He campaigned on the radio and in person for Bobby Killingsworth and also donated money to help cover his campaign expenses. He knew that if he could get Killingsworth elected, he would be able to keep the sheriff's tags and police equipment on his Cadillac.

Killingsworth, a good-natured individual, had become well known in the area through his appearances on the singer's weekly television show. For this reason, too, Bond felt that Killingsworth, who was a McNairy County native, had a better than average chance of winning the election.

*   *   *

A heavyset man, wearing a battered straw hat, blue denim shirt, and khaki pants strolled into the Anchor Club, located on a gravel road near the McNairy-Hardeman County line. The man ordered a beer and slid into a chair at a table next to Gordon Sparks, owner of the club.

"Who's going to win the sheriff's race, Gordon?" he asked.

"I think Clifford Coleman has the inside track."

"Huh. I thought Wendell Hicks was the front horse."

Sparks, in his late thirties, tall and slender with thinning dark hair, stood up. He kept a close eye on local happenings and had a good feel for the direction the county would take politically.

"Hicks may be gaining ground, but he sure as hell ain't leadin' the pack yet," Sparks said.

The man ordered another beer.

"Besides," Sparks added, "I'm more interested in the road commissioner's race right now. We need a new one. W.O. Watson believes too much in keeping the roads in their original condition to suit me.

"Look at this damned gravel road out in front of the place here. It's easy to tell when you leave Hardeman County and enter McNairy because the pavement ends and the dirt and gravel starts."

"Yeah, you're right, Gordon. We do need a new road commissioner. But I'm more concerned about the sheriff we get. You know the sheriff is the one who throws all us drunks into jail.

"I hate to see Buford Pusser leave office," the man added. "He was a fair man."

"People around here are really going to miss Buford when he turns in his badge," Sparks said. "Men like him are hard to find. He treated everyone like he wanted to be treated. I'm like you, I hate to see him go."

Gordon Sparks' prediction about the sheriff's race proved to be true. Coleman won by a substantial margin. And to his enjoyment, a new road commissioner was also elected.

In Adamsville, Buford Pusser was elected constable of the Third Civil District by more than eighty-four write-in votes. Raymond Gray, a farmer who was seeking reelection to the post, received sixty votes.

Pusser was surprised and honored that people in his hometown had thought enough of him to elect him constable when he had not even been a candidate.

In the state primary election, John Jay Hooker won the Democratic nomination for governor and Winfield Dunn received the Republican nod. Pusser was disappointed that Bill Jenkins didn't win Republican support, but he vowed to back his party's candidate all the way.

*   *   *

On August 31, 1970, Buford Pusser gathered up a few personal belongings in his hands, switched off the light, then strolled out the office door.

The next day, McNairy County would have a new sheriff, and the old one would be lounging around his house near a brightly painted city limits sign that read "WELCOME TO ADAMSVILLE . . . THE BIGGEST LITTLE TOWN IN TENNESSEE."

In the hallway of the basement near his office, Pusser met a newspaper man.

"Well, this is about it, isn't it sheriff?"

"Yeah. I've got three hours left as sheriff."

"What are you going to do now?"

"I don't have any special plans yet. For the time

being, I'm going to work on solving Pauline's murder case."

Pusser stared up the hallway.

"There are two killers running loose out there somewhere . . . and I'm going to find them. There were four men involved in the murder plot. Two are dead, and two are still alive. I know their identity."

"Who are they?" the reporter asked.

"I'd rather not say. I don't want them to know that I know who they are."

"I understand."

"Now, I'll be able to spend most of my time tracking down the two men. I'm going to see that they pay for the murder of my wife. It may take me awhile to find them, but I'll get them. This I promise!"

EPILOGUE

After he left office, Buford Pusser became active in the governor's race, spending all of his time campaigning for Winfield Dunn.

Pusser traveled more than ten thousand miles during a two-month period and spent endless hours urging Tennesseans to elect Dunn. He used his own money to cover the expenses of all of these trips.

At the Scenic Club in Knoxville, Pusser was a guest speaker at a $25-a-plate dinner and helped raise $25,000 for the campaign.

Most political observers predicted that Democratic nominee John Jay Hooker, Jr., who had been defeated four years before by Governor Buford Ellington, would soundly defeat Dunn, an unknown in Tennessee politics, but in the November election, Winfield Dunn defeated Hooker by several thousand votes.

Since Dunn's election, Buford Pusser has been associated with the governor's office.

Even though Bobby Killingsworth lost the McNairy County sheriff's race, Bond got his police-equipped automobile, but without official sheriff's tags. Pusser, however, arranged for Bond to be appointed police chief at Finger, a town of approximately 250 persons. Bond immediately purchased a new car, put special license plates on it and painted signs on the sides reading: "POLICE CHIEF, FINGER, TENNESSEE." Bond also had gold-embossed police certificates and commission cards printed and began handing them out freely to his friends.

Buford Pusser, when he is not working with Governor Dunn, is still searching for his wife's murderers. Most people think he will find them someday.